The Book of Margery Kempe
An Abridged Translation

Library of Medieval Women   ISSN 1369–9652

Series Editor: Jane Chance

The Library of Medieval Women aims to make available, in an English translation, significant works by, for, and about medieval women, from the age of the Church Fathers to the fifteenth century. The series encompasses many forms of writing, from poetry, visions, biography and autobiography, and letters to sermons, treatises and encyclopedias; the subject matter is equally diverse: theology and mysticism, classical mythology, medicine and science, history, hagiography, and instructions for anchoresses. Each text is presented with an introduction setting the material in context, a guide to further reading, and an interpretive essay.

We welcome suggestions for future titles in the series. Proposals or queries may be sent directly to the editor or publisher at the addresses given below; all submissions will receive prompt and informed consideration.

Professor Jane Chance, Department of English, MS 30, Rice University, PO Box 1892, Houston, TX 77251–1892, USA. E-mail: jchance@rice.edu

Boydell & Brewer Limited, PO Box 9, Woodbridge, Suffolk, IP12 3DF, UK. E-mail: boydell@boydell.co.uk. Website: www.boydell.co.uk

Previously published titles in this series appear at the back of this book

The Book of Margery Kempe
An Abridged Translation

Translated from the Middle English
with Introduction, Notes and Interpretive Essay

Liz Herbert McAvoy

University of Leicester

D.S. BREWER

First published 2003
D. S. Brewer, Cambridge

ISBN 0 85991 791 6

D. S. Brewer is an imprint of Boydell & Brewer Ltd
PO Box 9, Woodbridge, Suffolk IP12 3DF, UK
and of Boydell & Brewer Inc.
PO Box 41026, Rochester, NY 14604–4126, USA
website: www.boydell.co.uk

A catalogue record for this book is available
from the British Library

Library of Congress Cataloging-in-Publication Data
Kempe, Margery, b. ca. 1373.
  [Book of Margery Kempe. English. Selections]
  The book of Margery Kempe : an abridged translation / translated from
the Middle English with introduction, notes and interpretive essay by
Liz Herbert McAvoy.
     p. cm. – (Library of medieval women, ISSN 1369–9652)
Includes bibliographical references and index.
  ISBN 0–85991–791–6 (alk. paper)
1. Kempe, Margery, b. ca. 1373.   2. Authors, English – Middle English,
1100–1500 – Biography.   3. Christian pilgrims and pilgrimages – Early
works to 1800.   4. Women and literature – England – History – To 1500.
5. Christian women – Religious life – England.   6. Mysticism – England –
Early works to 1800.   I. Herbert McAvoy, Liz.   II. Title.   III. Series.
  PR2007.K4A199 2003
  248.2'2'092 – dc21   2003004451

This publication is printed on acid-free paper

Printed in Great Britain by
Athenæum Press Ltd, Gateshead, Tyne & Wear

Contents

Acknowledgements

I would like to express my gratitude in particular to Dr. Diane Watt, my former supervisor and colleague in the Department of English at the University of Wales, Aberystwyth, for her consistent and untiring support since 1996. Her advice and judgement have proved invaluable to me during the course of my pre- and post-doctoral activities, as has the impetus of her shared interests and enthusiasms. Thanks are also due to my other former colleagues in the Department, in particular Professor Lyn Pykett who continued to provide intellectual and material support for my research in the face of ubiquitous financial privation, and Joan Crawford and June Baxter whose secretarial help also contributed to the completion of this book. Finally and foremost, I am indebted to both friends and family for their huge enthusiasm for my work and their resigned acceptance of my long working days and protracted weekend absences over the course of the last six years.

List of Abbreviations

EETS	Early English Text Society
o.s.	Original Series
e.s.	Extra Series
s.s.	Special Series
MED	The Middle English Dictionary
OED	The Oxford English Dictionary

Introduction

> [N]othing can come to any conclusion when (women) share
> secrets, so proud and haughty are they, with such corrosive,
> venomous and harmful tongues.[1]

These words, uttered by Genius to Nature on the subject of women in Jean de Meun's infamous continuation of Guillaume de Lorris' allegorical poem *The Romance of the Rose*, echo a common misogynistic notion in the Middle Ages about the dangers attached to the female voice and incontinent body. Derived from authoritative biblical precedent, in particular the seduction of Adam by Eve's feminine charms in the Garden of Eden,[2] and adopted with great enthusiasm by the Church Fathers and other religious commentators, the theme of the seductive and uncontrollable voice of woman which permeated much of the literature of the medieval period and *The Book of Margery Kempe* in particular.[3] Indeed, it was reinforced by the teachings of Saint Paul who had famously proclaimed, 'I suffer not a woman to teach, nor to use authority over the man: but to be in silence';[4] such proscription constituted one of the principal barriers against women such as Margery Kempe confidently announcing their religious experiences alongside men and was, of course, one of the influences which also worked most effectively against female literacy and empowerment during the Middle Ages. Even the educated and relatively assured Julian of Norwich deemed it appropriate – in her early text at least – to defend her own act of writing in what amounts to a most self-conscious apologia:

> But God forbid that you should accuse me or think that I am
> a teacher, for I do not mean that to be the case. No I never

---

1   *The Romance of the Rose by Guillaume de Lorris and Jean de Meun*, ed. Charles Dahlberg (Princeton, 1971), pp. 280–1.
2   Genesis 3: 6.
3   All references to the original text will be taken from Margery Kempe, *The Book of Margery Kempe*, ed. Sandford Brown Meech and Hope Emily Allen, EETS o.s. 212 (London, New York & Toronto, 1997) and will be included in square brackets. References to the translations included in this volume will appear in round brackets.
4   I Timothy 2: 12.

meant that to be the case. For I am a woman, simple, feeble and frail.[5]

As this spirited interpolation would suggest, the act of writing for a woman was considered synonymous with teaching and preaching and as such constituted a similar misuse of the female voice and direct contravention of the proscriptions of Saint Paul and other patristic teachings.[6]

Moreover, the belief in woman's inability to control either voice or body was further reinforced by contemporary medical and anatomical theories which proclaimed her to be a naturally inferior being and possessor of a most dangerous body. Based on the teachings of the classical philosopher Aristotle, and modified and developed by the highly popular writings of the second-century philosopher and physician, Galen, women were considered to be naturally colder and wetter than the hot and dry male and, as a result, constantly craved union with men in order to modify their own inadequate temperatures.[7] One of the main consequences of this 'natural' disposition was that women were considered to be inherently – and dangerously – sexually voracious, and the link between the uncontrolled female voice and an insatiable sexual appetite was one which was forged time after time in medieval literature. We only have to go as far as Chaucer's garrulous, five-times married Wife of Bath and her famous pronouncement on husbands ('Blessed be God that I have married five!/ Welcome the sixth, whenever that shall be')[8] to find an example of this correlation between the female voice and female sexuality. Even the relatively tolerant theologian, Thomas Aquinas,

5   Julian of Norwich, *Revelations of Divine Love*, ed. Frances Beer (Heidelberg, 1978), pp. 47–8. The translation is my own. In her later text, known as the Long Text, Julian eradicates this apology for her female presumptuousness, possibly as a result of increased confidence in her own material after many years spent reworking and developing it. On the use of such a *topos* of humility by women writers in the Middle Ages see Barbara Newman, *Sister of Wisdom: Hildegarde's Theology of the Feminine* (Berkeley & Los Angeles, 1987), p. 2.

6   For a useful overview of patristic attitudes to the female voice see Rosalynn Voaden's study of female prophecy in the later Middle Ages, *God's Words, Women's Voices: The Discernment of Spirits in the Writing of Late-Medieval Women Visionaries* (York, 1999), pp. 7–40.

7   For a comprehensive study of sex difference in the Middle Ages as promulgated by popular medical and anatomical beliefs see Joan Cadden, *Meanings of Sex Difference in the Middle Ages: Medicine, Science and Culture* (Cambridge, 1993).

8   *The Riverside Chaucer*, ed. Larry Benson (Oxford, 1987), 'The Wife of Bath's Prologue', ll. 44–5. Again, the translation is my own.

writing in the thirteenth century, was to endorse the age-old need to police the female voice along with her sexuality. In an echo of earlier Pauline proscription, Aquinas advocates female silence

> . . . lest men's minds be enticed to lust . . . (and because) generally speaking women are not perfected in wisdom so as to be fit to be entrusted with public teaching.[9]

The extent to which such proscriptions had been absorbed into late-medieval socio-religious culture is everywhere attested to in *The Book of Margery Kempe*, and Margery Kempe's persistent attempts at contravening such proscriptive ideologies is the aspect of her self-representation and her writing which has most arrested, perplexed or infuriated her audience in turn – both during her own lifetime and in more recent times. The extracts chosen for translation in this current volume, therefore, serve to reflect some of these ideologies at play as well as revealing the methods employed by Margery, the *Book*'s main protagonist and attributed author, to overturn them and attain a measure of autonomy.

The Book of Margery Kempe constitutes a unique and riveting account of the progress of a woman's spiritual and intellectual growth within the context of a mercantile and status-conscious East Anglia during the early fifteenth century, ranging from the days of her youth to her old age. The narrative, opening with an account of its protagonist's marriage, the birth of her first child and her subsequent physical and spiritual crisis, proceeds to document Margery Kempe's early sinfulness, her thwarted religious calling and protracted journey towards a desired goal of spiritual perfection. During the course of this arduous journey she will forge a vow of chastity with her husband soon after the birth of her fourteenth child, embark upon a series of pilgrimages, both in England and abroad (one of which involves a pivotal visit to the Holy Land), and be subject to a series of arrests for what her peers frequently regard as socially aberrant behaviour. Much of the narrative too will concern itself with an almost obsessive search for endorsement of her religious calling by means of urgent consultation with a long series of ecclesiastics and other holy men and women. Not only does Margery tell of a visit to Julian of Norwich in 1413 (92–4), for example, but she also recounts a visit to Thomas Arundel, archbishop of Canterbury, who appears to

---

9   Thomas Aquinas, *Summa Theologiae, 2a2ae, qu. 171–8*, ed. and trans. R. Potter OP, vol. 45 (London, 1970), pp. 133–5.

fully approve of her religious practices ('he found no fault with her but approved her way of life' [37]). Similarly, she appears to enjoy contact with other well-known figures in the Church: both Philip Repingdon, bishop of Lincoln, for example, and her own confessor, Robert Spryngolde, offer her considerable support, and references to Spryngolde in particular (who will later become her primary confessor) punctuate the text at regular intervals. In fact, the relationships which she forges with people of established spiritual authority are far more vividly delineated in the text than those existing between herself and her family, who seem to take a back-seat and often disappear from her narrative altogether, pointing towards the *Book*'s ultimate purpose which is, as clearly announced at its onset, to invoke 'sinful wretches, so that they may have great solace and comfort and understanding of the high and unspeakable mercy of our sovereign Saviour, Jesus Christ' [1].

Margery's relationships with figures of authority, however, are not always as positive and affirming. On the contrary, much of the narrative is taken up with the documentation of groundswells of antipathy and antagonism directed at her by a whole succession of priests and other figures of male authority who fail to recognise the special grace to which she believes she is privy. On a number of occasions, for example, she is arrested and arraigned for heresy and other transgressive behaviour – the wearing of white clothes, for example, and travelling without her husband – in front of a full ecclesiastic court at Leicester, York and Beverley whilst on pilgrimage in the north of England. At other times she is vilified by visiting preachers in her own church in King's Lynn (formerly Bishop's Lynn) and forced out of the religious community because of her eccentric and noisy expressions of piety. Such ambivalent and paradoxical relationships between Margery and representatives of the Church are never fully resolved in her text, although as she gets older it is evident that she develops increasingly effective strategies for dealing with them, many of which are based upon her own experiences of being a wife and a mother – as will be demonstrated further in the interpretive essay included in this volume. Moreover, her motherhood, her sexual experiences and the increasingly authoritative use of her female voice eventually combine to provide her with a set of matrixes to aid her on her journey towards spiritual perfection and facilitate the creation of a permanent record of that journey in the form of a written text in which the female body frequently acts as primary metaphor and exemplar.

However, Margery Kempe also recognises the necessity of the

male clergy for public endorsement of her vocation as holy woman,[10] an imperative which is the source of much tension in the text, although it also remains the case that the authority to which Margery turns most often and upon which she is most heavily reliant is that of Christ himself, drawn from the many personal conversations which she enjoys with him during their visionary encounters. Instigated by his early appearance at her bedside following a bout of psychological and physical illness, the intimate relationship which Margery develops with him not only intensifies the authority of her personal devotions, but also provides her with an authoritative means of circumventing much ecclesiastic proscription and prohibition, ultimately offering her a route towards what is ostensibly a form of spiritual and bodily freedom. It is therefore fitting that the *Book* should end with a series of prayers which not only embody and exemplify her long-desired authority as holy woman, but also offer thanks to God for the suffering which she has undergone – and will continue to undergo – in the achievement of this end.

Manuscript history and reception

The only extant manuscript containing Margery Kempe's narrative in its entirety dates from sometime before 1450[11] and, although not the original one begun in 1436 and produced by Margery's own scribe, it is possibly an early – even a direct – copy of the original. Comprised of 124 leaves, the manuscript bears at the foot of its last page the scribal signature of somebody called Salthows, whom earlier scholars have traced to a probable East Anglian provenance.[12] Moreover, in this manuscript the book remains untitled – the treatise's now accepted title is a product of twentieth-century scholarship and based upon an inscription at the head of an early sixteenth-century redacted version of the text (about which I will say more later) which identifies its origin as being 'the boke of Margerie kempe of lynn' (127). Also at the head of this redaction there appears an attribution of book ownership to the priory of Mount Grace ('This

---

10 On the role of the male clergy in the construction of the orthodox holy woman, see Voaden, *God's Words, Women's Voices*, op. cit. On Margery Kempe in particular, see pp. 109–54.

11 Having been acquired by the British Library in 1980, the manuscript – which is probably an early copy of Margery's original text and not the one originally written down by her scribe – is now known as London, British Library Additional Manuscript 61823.

12 On this see Meech and Allen, *Book*, p. xxxiii.

boke is of Mountegrace'), that is to say the Carthusian monastery of Mount Grace near East Harlsey, eight miles north of Northallerton in Yorkshire. Marginal annotation within the redaction manuscript also points towards Mount Grace ownership: Richard Methley, for example, who was a Carthusian monk at that house, is mentioned by name by one annotator, as is John Norton, who was Prior there at the same time as Methley in the late fifteenth century. Both Methley and Norton, as the annotations also suggest, like Margery, also claimed to be privy to mystical visions – something which goes some way to explaining why this unique manuscript should find its way into this house of Carthusian monks where it was evidently highly valued.[13] Subsequently, the manuscript appears to have gone missing and did not re-emerge until 1934 when it was discovered in the library of one Colonel Butler-Bowden; indeed, two bookplates serve to identify the manuscript as having been the property of his own family from at least 1754.

Thus, before this chance discovery of this long-forgotten text, our limited knowledge of *The Book of Margery Kempe* and its proclaimed author had been gleaned from the redaction as the only extant source available. This radically dismantled and reconstructed version of the original (translated here in an appendix to this volume), first printed by Wynkyn de Worde in 1501, reprinted by Henry Pepwell in 1521, and edited in the twentieth century by Edmund Gardner,[14] was the text which had led this first modern editor to speculate of its author:

> The revelations show that she was (or had been) a woman of some wealth and social position, who had abandoned the world to become an ancress . . . [I]t is enough to show that she was a worthy precursor of that other great woman mystic of East Anglia: Juliana of Norwich.[15]

---

[13] For a discussion of Carthusian enthusiasm for this type of mystical work see Marleen Cré, 'Women in the Charterhouse? Julian of Norwich's *Revelations of Divine Love* and Marguerite Porete's *Mirror of Simple Souls* in British Library, MS Additional 37790', in Denis Renevey and Christiania Whitehead (eds), *Writing Religious Women: Female Spiritual and Textual Practices in Late Medieval England* (Cardiff, 2000), pp. 43–62, especially p. 46.

[14] Edmund D. Gardner, *The Cell of Self-Knowledge: Seven Early English Mystical Treatises Printed by Henry Pepwell in 1521* (London & New York, 1910). Subsequently, the redacted text has also been reproduced in Meech & Allen, *Book*, pp. 353–7.

[15] Gardner, *Cell of Self Knowledge*, pp. xx–xxi.

Such reconstructive guesswork on the part of Gardner was necessitated by the fact that this version of the text excises all the apparently autobiographical material pertinent to Margery's life. References to her excessive religious practices, for example – the crying, the screaming, the frequent loss of bodily control and the multiple physical collapses, all of which dominate the original *Book* itself – are virtually non-existent. Instead, the redacted text is constituted of a series of decontextualised and dechronologised conversations between Margery and Christ, providing a misleading dialogic narrative which reconstructs Margery Kempe as far more orthodox a holy woman and far less physical a presence than she appears in the original text. This is, perhaps, best illustrated in the opening exchange between Christ and Margery in this truncated text which has Christ profess:

[E]ven if you were to say a thousand *Our Fathers* every day, you should not please me as well as you do when you are in silence and allow me to speak to you in your soul (127).

It would seem here that this redactor would have even Christ adhere to the old adage that the most exemplary of women is the one who remains silent. In effect, then, by making use of this passage to construct part of the introit to his text, the redactor clearly lays out his own agenda for his audience. It is therefore hardly surprising that this version then proceeds to transform Margery Kempe entirely from the self-confessed loquacious and worldly woman whom we see at the forefront of the original text into one who has been successfully controlled and effectively silenced. Moreover, and as if to consolidate this strategic transformation, by the time the Pepwell version of this redaction came to print in 1521, Margery had completed her final metamorphosis into 'devout anchoress of Lynn' (131, n.9), the title by which this version of the treatise is introduced. Ironically, it was in such a state of double enclosure that both woman and her text were to remain for another four hundred years.

After such high expectations of the original text generated by this redaction, it was with some scholarly disappointment that the discovery of the full-length version of the *Book* was greeted in the twentieth century, and the critic, Herbert Thurston, in his knee-jerk response to the contents of the full text, was fairly typical of the critical dismay with which both book and author were greeted. Writing in 1936, Thurston proclaimed of Margery:

If she had really been an ancress, living secluded in her cell, these peculiarities would not have mattered. But she insisted on going everywhere, following, as she believed, the special call of God.[16]

Indeed, 'secluded' was not an adjective which could readily be applied to the Margery Kempe who emerged from the folios of this elusive manuscript, and her self-revelation as noisy, dramatic, affective and highly emotional woman was to send many of her twentieth-century commentators into confusion and disarray. Critics were split as to whether Margery could now qualify as a mystic at all, preferring to brand her as 'hysteric' rather than recognise her as woman visionary, forged along the lines of other, established women visionaries.[17] Echoing the response of the ecclesiastic courts at Leicester, York and Beverley, one twentieth-century critic even saw fit to define Margery's singular expression of nuptial mysticism in terms of 'sexual aberrance'.[18] For a while, then, Margery seemed doomed to be re-interred into that same stone-walled realm of repression from which she had so recently emerged.

However, upon the rapid and inexorable development from the early 1970s onwards of a feminist approach to literature within academic circles – and within medieval studies in particular – there came about a welcome upsurge of interest in this singularly rich and provocative text; and it is an interest and enthusiasm which has been gaining momentum ever since.[19] Far from being a literary disappointment, it is now regarded as one of the most electrifying and authoritative accounts of how a woman was able to circumvent contemporary socio-religious proscription and forge for herself, in spite of seemingly insurmountable obstacles, a life which incorporated a measure of both autonomy and personal fulfilment. As a result, *The Book of Margery Kempe* has now found its way onto a

[16] Herbert Thurston, 'Review', *Tablet* (1936), p. 570.
[17] For an overview of negative critical attitudes towards Margery Kempe see Eluned Bremner, 'Margery Kempe and the Critics: Disempowerment and Deconstruction', in Sandra J. McEntire (ed.), *Margery Kempe: A Book of Essays* (New York & London, 1992), pp. 117–35.
[18] T. W. Coleman, *English Mystics of the Fourteenth Century* (London, 1938), p. 175.
[19] The conglomeration of feminist readings of the *Book* are too many to mention here, but perhaps the most significant have been Clarissa Atkinson, *Mystic and Pilgrim: The Book and World of Margery Kempe* (Ithaca, 1983); Lynn Staley, *Margery Kempe's Dissenting Fictions* (Pennsylvania, 1984); Karma Lochrie, *Margery Kempe and Translations of the Flesh* (Philadelphia, 1991); Diane Watt, *Secretaries of God: Women Prophets in Late Medieval and Early Modern England* (Cambridge, 1997).

large majority of medieval literature courses within the Academy
and has come very close to taking on canonical status.

Questions of Authorship and Authority

In spite of its increasing popularity, however, it is true to say that the
Book remains subject to intense critical debate – a debate which
rages primarily around complex questions of authorship and veracity.
Indeed, scholars continue to remain divided about the extent to
which the text can even be considered to be the work of Margery
Kempe at all, given the evident input of a series of male scribes to the
work. The text itself is prefaced by a *Proem* which is attributed to
Margery's amanuensis and which documents the difficult process by
which Margery Kempe came to writing. Here is recounted, for
example, the death of her first scribe (who had not set to writing until
nearly twenty years after Margery was first urged by a confessor to
document her mystical experiences) and the subsequent hiatus whilst
two more priests attempted to read his illegible handwriting and
make sense of his poor grasp of the English language. Finally, after
an initial rejection of the task, the final amanuensis documents how,
as a result of divine grace (and more pertinently, perhaps, a pair of
spectacles), he found that he was able to understand perfectly the
writing of the first scribe and continue with the work in hand. As a
result, he tells us how he set about re-writing Book 1 (in which is
recorded Margery's life from the moment of her marriage in about
1393 until the *Book*'s inception in 1436), then proceeding to record
the material documented in Book 2, which concerns itself primarily
with the conversion of an aberrant son and Margery's own journey to
Europe during her old age.

The fact that Margery was highly dependent upon her scribes to
bring her book into being is beyond debate and many critics have
argued that this male collaboration with Margery seriously under-
mines the integrity of the *Book* as female authored.[20] Indeed, for one
recent critic, *The Book of Margery Kempe* remains a text 'written by

[20] See, in particular, Anthony E. Goodman, 'The Piety of John Brunham's
Daughter, of Lynn', in *Medieval Women*, ed. Derek Baker (Oxford, 1978), who
argues for the scribe's shaping of the *Book*, pp. 348–9. Similarly, John C. Hirsch
considers much of the *Book's* content to be the work of the second scribe in
'Author and Scribe in *The Book of Margery Kempe*', *Medium Aevum* 44 (1975),
pp. 145–50. More recently, Rosalynn Voaden has asserted, 'It is obvious that at
least three people are writing this book, and none of them is particularly good at
it.' *God's Words, Women's Voices*, p. 113.

men, for men and about men'.[21] Such a reading, however, threatens to descend newly into the realm of the reactionary in its lack of emphasis placed on the considerable wealth of evidence to the contrary found within the *Book* itself. Far from asserting his stamp of authority, for example, in fact Margery's amanuensis is always at pains to efface his own contribution, telling us things like 'he read every word of it over to this creature, and she sometimes helped him where there was any difficulty' (103). On a number of other occasions too he emphasises that the *Book* is 'truly recorded' [220] and written 'according to her (Margery's) own tongue' [221]. Indeed, this scribe consistently downgrades his own role in the text's construction as being secondary, even going so far on occasion to include some personal material which depicts him as both naïve and foolish in his inability to fully trust Margery's prophetic gifts and affective responses. Ultimately, and in spite of his own undertaking of the physical act of writing, he is insistent in his desire to attribute the act of composition to Margery. Indeed, as Michael Clanchy has famously recognised, for many medieval writers the act of writing was a speech act rather than an activity undertaken with pen in hand,[22] something which is nowhere better reflected in the scribe's account of the *Book*'s inception:

> This book is not written in order, everything following one after the other as it happened, but as the matter came to the creature's mind when it was to be written down. For it was so long before it was written down that she had forgotten the time and the order when things happened (103).

In other words, the scribe is most insistent here that the text reflects accurately the information proffered by Margery Kempe, its author, precisely because of the chronological and structural inconsistencies which have arisen because of the time-lapse between the events themselves and this act of recording them. If we take this profession at face value, in many ways *The Book of Margery Kempe* can be said to reverberate with the voice of its female author which, in turn, is endorsed in this way by her own male amanuensis. Whatever our position on this as readers, however, the debate surrounding this

---

21 Sarah Rees-Jones, ' "A peler of Holy Cherch": Margery Kempe and the Bishops', in Jocelyn Wogan-Browne (ed.), *Medieval Women: Texts and Contexts in Late Medieval Britain* (Turnhout, 2000), pp. 377–91 (391).

22 M. T. Clanchy, *From Memory to Written Record: England 1066–1307* (Oxford & Cambridge, Mass., repr. 1993), pp. 125–6.

issue is entirely symptomatic of the complexity of this intriguing text and, more pertinently perhaps, the difficulties of bringing into being and defining any female-authored text during this period and beyond.

The *Book* in its socio-religious context

Whatever the truth of its authorship, *The Book of Margery Kempe* – as Edmund Gardner had accurately speculated – reveals in its protagonist a woman born into a fairly affluent and influential family within the prosperous town of Bishop's Lynn in Norfolk, probably some time in 1373. Contemporary records reveal that her father, John Brunham, held the office of mayor of Lynn no less than five times between 1370 and 1391 and was also one of the two members of parliament returned by the town for varying periods during the twenty years between 1364 and 1384.[23] In her early, much more worldly years before her conversion, Margery tells us that she had taken great pride in the elevated status which this social position offered her locally. Indeed, she documents early in the *Book* how much she enjoyed parading around her wealth and status in a highly conspicuous display, insisting on wearing the most ostentatious and elaborate fashions of the day and being consumed by the sin of pride [9]. Moreover, the opening passages of the *Book*, with their preoccupation with the tensions created by the collision of the new monetary values of an up-and-coming mercantile middle class with the old values of a strictly hierarchical feudal society, re-enact perfectly – and with intense realism – the anxieties which Langland and Chaucer were also busy recording at the same time as Margery was displaying herself and her wealth in the busy mercantile centre of Bishop's Lynn.

Such social anxieties and tensions had been further exacerbated by the fact that during the last decades of the fourteenth century the country had been experiencing a period of considerable socio-economic change. The Black Death of mid century had severely depleted the population by up to fifty percent in some areas. As a result, what has been identified as a mid-century crisis ensued which not only led to a population deficit but also to a decline in the demand for certain commodities within the marketplace.[24] However,

---

23 The relevant documents have been included as an appendix in Meech and Allen, *Book*, pp. 359–62.
24 For a detailed account of these sociological changes in the fourteenth century see

at the same time, the urban centres had become subject to increased productivity, leading to the depopulation of the rural areas by people flocking to the towns for the variety of opportunities available there. This increased opportunity is, perhaps, also reflected early in Margery Kempe's narrative when she documents her own attempts at setting up firstly a brewing business and then a horse-mill [9–10]. According to Margery's own confession, however, each attempt was doomed to failure because of her blind adherence to superficial monetary values and materialism, rather than putting her trust in God. Indeed, even after her religious conversion and the onset of her mystical experiences, Margery's narrative continues to reflect the mercantile and mercenary ethics of urban society, and the prevailing sense of commodification within all aspects of English urban life results in a persistent anxiety which pervades her text.

It is no coincidence, then, that Margery's narrative begins with the representation of her own body as a commodity which is offered in marriage to a man whom she confesses to having considered her social inferior. John Kempe was a local merchant whose family also appears in contemporary records,[25] although they never seem to have reached the level of distinction of Margery's own family. In fact – and echoing Chaucer's generic depiction of his own pilgrim-merchant who, although a 'worthy man', is also secretly in debt[26] – John Kempe is characteristically represented as being in debt, eventually relying upon Margery to pay off his creditors. The birth of their first child soon after this marriage – 'as nature would have it' (31) – intensifies the sense of Margery's own bodily commodification, and proves to be the catalyst for a redefinition of self, as I suggested previously, which will involve her leaving the family home and embarking upon an attempt to forge an autonomous, independent existence as holy woman and tread the frequently hazardous path towards spiritual 'perfection'.

Such an uncompromising inclusion of herself at the forefront of her own narrative has resulted in The Book of Margery Kempe frequently being hailed as the first autobiography written in English.[27] However, this appraisal is problematised firstly by the

---

R. H. Britnell, The Commercialisation of English Society, 1000–1500 (Cambridge, 1993), pp. 155–78.

[25] Meech and Allen, Book, pp. 362–8.

[26] Benson (ed.), Riverside Chaucer, pp. 27–8, ll. 270–84.

[27] See, for example, Clarissa Atkinson, Mystic and Pilgrim: The Book and World of Margery Kempe (Ithaca, 1983), p. 14, and Barry Windeatt (ed.), The Book of

aforementioned debate surrounding authorship and authenticity, and secondly by more controversial readings of this text such as that proffered by Lynn Staley, for example.[28] Staley, who regards this text as a work of fiction in which Kempe, the author, constructs an imaginary protagonist, Margery, as a means of critiquing current religious and social practices and injustices, points out that the *Book*'s structure is, in fact, based upon the biographical tradition of saints' *Lives* so popular in the later Middle Ages. These works were often characterised by a formulaic moment of religious calling or conversion, often in childhood, followed by a subsequent struggle to reach a state of spiritual perfection or transcendence. The *Book* clearly attempts to adhere to this authoritative pattern – albeit very loosely – and its hagiographic elements are further enhanced by the fact that it is written in the third person throughout, its author referring to herself consistently as 'this creature'.[29] For Staley, the incursion of the male amanuensis into the text thus becomes a trope to lend authority to this female-authored work of fiction. Whether we align ourselves alongside Staley and this challenging and innovative reading or remain more sceptical, Margery's self-depiction as a 'creature' can nevertheless be acknowledged as an attempt to imitate the style adopted by the male authors of traditional saints' *Lives* and imbue what is an intensely subjective narrative with a measure of objectivity and authority.

At this time in the fifteenth century, of course, vernacular translations of the *Vitae* of saints – particularly the virgin saints – were highly popular amongst the laity, and amongst a newly literate female audience in particular.[30] Margery's text is punctuated with

---

Margery Kempe (Harlow, 2000), Introduction, p. 1. For a longer discussion of this aspect of the *Book* see Janel M. Mueller, 'Autobiography of a New "Creatur": Female Spirituality, Selfhood, and Authorship in *The Book of Margery Kempe*', in *Women in the Middle Ages and the Renaissance*, ed. Mary Beth Rose (Syracuse, 1986), pp. 155–82.

28 Staley, *Dissenting Fictions*, op. cit. For a discussion of the *Book* as a social text, see Kathleen Ashley, 'Historicizing Margery: *The Book of Margery Kempe* as Social Text', *Journal of Medieval and Early Modern Studies* 28 (1998), pp. 371–88.

29 There are, however, several occasions when Margery – or her scribe – reverts to using the first person, probably accidentally. These are to be found in Meech & Allen, *Book*, pp. 14, 34, 44, 214, 230.

30 Particularly popular were those penned by Jacobus de Voragine in his *Legenda Aurea* in the thirteenth century and its fifteenth-century translation, the *Gilte Legende*. For a recent edition of a selection of these *Lives* see Richard Hamer and Vida Russell, *Supplementary Lives in Some Manuscripts of the Gilte Legende*,

references to the popular virgin saints Katherine and Margaret, for example (Margaret was also the patron saint of Margery's own parish church in Bishop's Lynn), and it is evident that these virgin saints are ones with whom Margery identified in no small measure. Similarly, in other contexts Margery draws upon the example of a series of married and maternal saints to lend authority to her calling. In particular, Saint Bridget, the Swedish saint who was canonised in Margery's own lifetime and who like Margery had been both a wife and a mother, provides a major role-model for Margery, both as putative holy woman and as author – something I will return to later. Other married and maternal saints are also alluded to in the text in what appear to constitute strategic interpolations by Margery's scribe in order to enhance her credibility and underscore his own initial lack of faith in her singularity and bodily excesses. One of these, Marie d'Oignies (d. 1213), was a holy woman also renowned for her extraordinary gift of tears and for other equally dramatic mystical displays; another is Elizabeth of Hungary (canonised in 1235) who, like Margery, entered the holy life after marriage and children.[31] Such well-established exemplars of authoritative holy women stand alongside the ubiquitous Virgin and Mary Magdalene in the *Book* and comprise part of the whole panoply of alternative religious female authorities invoked within this text in an attempt to further validate both Margery's life and her female act of writing. Yet, whereas the saint's *Life* tends to be characterised by the male perspective on acceptable and desirable expressions of female religiosity, *The Book of Margery Kempe* is unique in its depiction of a medieval Englishwoman's life and religious practices as told from the perspective of the female subject herself, whatever the level of mediation supplied by her male amanuensis.

Margery's scribe's initial scepticism to Margery's claims and her bodily excesses provides a paradigm for public response to her in her

EETS o.s. 315 (Oxford, 2000). See also the writing of Margery's East Anglian contemporary, Osborn Bokenham, *Legendys of Hooly Wummen* (c. 1447). For a translated edition of these stories see Sheila Delany (ed. & trans.), *A Legend of Holy Women* (Notre Dame & London, 1992).

31 On Elizabeth of Hungary and on maternal saints generally see Clarissa Atkinson, *The Oldest Vocation: Christian Motherhood in the Middle Ages* (Ithaca, 1991), especially pp. 165–70; see also Barbara Newman, *From Virile Woman to WomanChrist: Studies on Medieval Religion and Literature* (Philadelphia, 1995), pp. 76–101.

own lifetime, in spite of the fact that she was operating within a culture which generally exercised a high degree of tolerance – indeed, actively encouraged – extravagant bodily re-enactment of the scriptures. Late-medieval affective interpretations of biblical narrative had been promoted and popularised in part by the highly emotive and corporeal treatment of the Passion by the thirteenth-century Franciscan monk now known as Pseudo-Bonaventure. His popular treatise, *Meditationes Vitae Christi* (which had been translated into the English vernacular by Nicholas Love in the early fifteenth century), may well have been one of the texts which had an influence upon Margery, and was characterised by two main features of affective spirituality: firstly an intensely realised sense of the corporeal, and secondly, a fixation upon and imitation of Christ's suffering in all its humanity. Here the medieval subject was called upon to continually contemplate – and ultimately perform – the sufferings and privations of Christ in order to reach a deeper level of understanding of its spiritual and corporeal implications. The contemplative reader was asked also to conform to all aspects of Christ's life and figuratively suffer his death and resurrection within his/her own life. For many – and particularly within a monastic context – this was frequently expressed by means of self-denigration, self-denial, self-abuse. In other scenarios, however, the contemplative could be overcome by seemingly involuntary expressions of *imitatio* [imitation] which were characterised by tears, loud cryings, bodily contortions, and – as in the case of Saint Francis of Assisi – stigmata. As far as Margery Kempe is concerned, her own *imitatio Christi* [imitation of Christ] seems to have been an amalgam of both the voluntary and involuntary, both conforming to and entirely outdoing contemporary expressions of this particular form of piety. What is particularly important in the case of Margery's *imitatio*, however, is that it is deeply informed by her own specifically female bodily experiences: re-enactment of childbirth agonies becomes an expression of the salvific suffering of the crucifix; sexual gratification becomes a statement of the ecstasy of mystical union; and her monstrous and ungoverned female voice becomes a privileged medium for ventriloquising the word of God, all of which are clearly reflected in the extracts selected for translation in this current volume. Time after time, in the face of a failure to achieve authority by orthodox means, Margery has recourse to the experiences of her own body and its female specificity in order to forge an alternative – and feminine – route to religious expression and salvation, and it is such an insistence upon the articulacy of the female body and its specific experiences which provides yet another piece of evidence for attributing the *Book*'s authorship to Margery herself, of course.

Margery and the Lollard threat

During the time when Margery Kempe was at her most visible and vociferous, the Church had begun to confront the only significant heretical threat to religious orthodoxy experienced in England during the Middle Ages – a heterodox movement which became known as Lollardy.[32] The Lollard heresy had emerged from the university at Oxford in the 1380s and had been inspired by the teaching of the theologian, John Wycliffe, who died in 1384. Followers of Wycliffe, in the form of wandering preachers, began to promulgate his ideas during the 1380s and into the 1390s, infiltrating in particular into parts of central and southern England. By the early fifteenth century, Lollardy had gained a firm foothold, particularly amongst the gentrified classes and within academia. Following the climax of the revolt against the monarchy by the arch-Lollard, John Oldcastle (whose daughter Margery is accused of being during a particularly difficult trial at Beverley in the north of England; 85–91), the heresy became associated primarily with the bourgeoisie and artisans – the very level of society in which Margery was living and operating during that period. It would also appear from contemporary records of heresy trials during the early fifteenth century that Lollardy was particularly well-established in East Anglia, although not so much so in the north of England. This, of course, is probably the reason for the high level of paranoia about Margery's potential as a Lollard which she encounters during her pilgrimage to the north of England and her arrests in 1417.

The Lollard doctrine had originated as a critique of orthodox religious practices and beliefs, and promoted the primacy of scripture as the ultimate religious authority. It sought to by-pass the clergy as being at best irrelevant and distracting, at worst corrupt and corrupting. Similarly, it rejected the use of oaths and swearing, and wholly denied the doctrine of transubstantiation – the process by which the bread on the altar was mystically transformed into the body of Christ during the Mass. Some branches of the heresy also

---

[32] The definitive text on the Lollard movement in England is Anne Hudson, *The Premature Reformation: Wycliffite Texts and Lollard History* (Oxford & New York, 1988). See also Shannon McSheffery, *Gender and Heresy: Women and Men in Lollard Communities, 1420–1530* (Philadelphia, 1995) for an important examination of the gendered implications of the heresy in England.

queried the validity of other sacraments such as marriage, and in this context it is significant that on a number of occasions Margery is interrogated vigorously on both these sacramental issues by ecclesiastic authority.

By the time that Margery herself became subject to accusations of Lollardy, however, the term had been coined as a type of 'catch-all' phrase which served to define a multiplicity of aberrancies – be they religious, social or sexual. As a consequence, we find Margery being addressed as both whore and Lollard in the same breath on a variety of occasions, accusations which would probably have remained harmless had Archbishop Arundel of Canterbury not introduced his infamous statute, the *De Heretico Comburendo* of 1401, which legislated for the burning of heretics. In fact, the statute was in part introduced specifically to allow for the burning of one William Sawtrey, then a heterodox priest in London, but formerly parish priest of Margery's own church in Bishop's Lynn. Sawtrey had been arrested for Lollardy on a number of occasions and was finally burned at the stake at Smithfield in March 1401. It is with some seriousness, then, that we must consider Margery's own position when confronted by the threat of burning, both at Canterbury after a heated confrontation with the monks there [27–9] and in Beverley in Yorkshire where she is held under house arrest following earlier arraignment at York (85–91). Margery's likely former association with Sawtrey (although nowhere documented in the *Book*), allied to the persistent accusations of religious and personal heterodoxy to which she is subject, presents her readers with an intriguing web of association between herself and the Lollard heresy which, in spite of her denials of any adherence herself, was clearly a major grey area which she perpetually risked occupying in her attempts to forge an independent, spiritual life for herself. As contemporary records reveal, with its emphasis on the scriptures in the vernacular and its enthusiastic embracing of a vernacular book culture, Lollardy had certainly produced some well-informed women in the fifteenth century,[33] a category in which, in spite of her professions to the contrary, one would have to include Margery Kempe. As we have seen, she was familiar with a variety of saints' *Lives* and the writing of Pseudo-Bonaventure, as well as a variety of popular devotional and mystical texts also written in the vernacular – the works of Richard

---

[33] On this see Margaret Aston, 'Lollard Women Priests?', *Journal of Ecclesiastical History* 31, 4 (October 1980), pp. 441–61 (443).

Rolle, for instance, and Walter Hilton.[34] It is also possible that she had access to a vernacular Bible (something which was still outlawed except on licence during this period), or else glossed copies or accounts of the Gospels in English – and she is also given to talking perpetually about religious matters. Her prolific knowledge of the scriptures is also something which subjects her to further accusations of Lollardy – during her arrest at Leicester, for example – but at other times secures her the admiration of senior churchmen, Archbishop Arundel included, as we have seen. Whether firmly rooted within orthodoxy or moving into the blurred domain which constituted heresy, however, it remains the case that Margery's beliefs and her uncategorisable self frequently enable her to out-argue and success-fully overcome the strictures of patriarchal ideology which are continually placed in her way, both at home and abroad.

Late-medieval pilgrimage and religious controversy

Following her release from domestic constraints after the birth of her last child in 1413, Margery embarks upon the first of her series of arduous pilgrimages. Already a seasoned traveller – her vow of chas-tity with John Kempe is negotiated whilst returning from pilgrimage to York and she has already made multiple visits to Norwich and one to Canterbury – her need to travel now takes on almost compulsive status. Her most significant and life-changing pilgrimage, of course, is that undertaken to the locations of the Passion in Jerusalem but there are also other equally difficult journeys to be made – to Santiago de Compostela in Spain, for example (about which Margery is unusually reticent, offering no information beyond the assertion that she went there); a dangerous tour of the north Midlands and Yorkshire; and finally, in advanced old age, a last problematic trip to Prussia with her recently bereaved daughter-in-law. Wherever her journey, however, the problems which she encounters bear the same characteristics: not only is she continually confronted by situa-tions of intense physical danger, she is perpetually subject to accusa-tions of hypocrisy and frequently abandoned or ostracised by her

---

[34] In fact, Margery alludes to Rolle's popular mystical work, *Incendium Amoris* on three occasions, and it seems to have had an influence on some of her more lyrical depictions of her mystical experiences. The work of Hilton's to which she refers on two occasions is his *Scale of Perfection*, another highly popular contemporary text, although laying down very different guidelines for desirable contemplative practices from those adhered to by Margery.

fellow pilgrims who object to her pious stance on the subject of pilgrimage. In this sense, the *Book* stands as a remarkable contribution to the so-called 'pilgrimage debate' which was raging during the late fourteenth and early fifteenth centuries, and gives clear insight into the effect that this debate had on the lives of ordinary people.

By the time that Margery began on her itinerant schedule in the early 1400s, the subject of pilgrimage had become the locus of considerable religious controversy and it was subject to intense debate within both orthodox and heterodox circles.[35] Since the influence of the Church Fathers first began to be felt, pilgrimage had long been accepted as a devotional activity and – more importantly – provided a suitably accessible metaphor for the human condition and its relationship with God. In the fourth century, for example, Saint Ambrose had spoken in terms of human existence as a three-tiered pilgrimage during which the Christian wandered the figurative desert of the world searching for redemption in the hope of realising salvation and Paradise. On the other hand, Ambrose's contemporary, Saint Augustine, identified life on earth as a figurative pilgrimage which could lead a person either towards the heavenly Jerusalem (Paradise) or else to the fleshly and corrupt pit of Babylon (Hell). The choice of road taken was the pilgrim's own.[36] Similar concerns about the ideology and symbolism of physical pilgrimage was echoed in much of the literature of the late Middle Ages. Besides the obvious example of Chaucer's *Canterbury Tales*, at the end of the fourteenth century Langland was also to shape the visionary text of *Piers Plowman* according to the moral progress upon which the ideology of pilgrimage was predicated. The metaphorical or symbolic nature of pilgrimage was even more explicitly delineated in an anonymous treatise written in about 1400 entitled *A Myrour to Lewde Men and Wymmen* [A Mirror to Ignorant Men and Women], a work written to meet the increase in demand for vernacular works of piety during

[35] On medieval pilgrimage in a wider European context see Jonathan Sumption, *Pilgrimage: An Image of Mediaeval Religion* (London, 1975). See also Norbert Ohler, *The Medieval Traveller*, trans. Caroline Hillier (Woodbridge, 1989) for a fascinating insight into the physical details of pilgrimage and travel in the Middle Ages. Also particularly helpful on the subject of pilgrimage is Diana Webb, *Pilgrims and Pilgrimage in Medieval Europe* (London, 1999).
[36] For a useful overview of these and other attitudes towards pilgrimage and of the pilgrimage controversy see Peter Brown, *Chaucer at Work: The Making of the Canterbury Tales* (London & New York, 1994), especially pp. 16–23.

this period. In this treatise, the author voices the same ideological concerns as exemplified by these earlier authors when he asserts:

> For it is true that all of mankind in this world is in exile and wilderness. He is exiled from his native land, like a pilgrim or a wayfarer in a strange land where in no way may he abide; but each day, every hour and continually he must needs pass on his way.[37]

Moreover, the author goes on to assert the necessity of the true Christian's desire to make this journey, and thus its physical expression on earth is promoted as both a desirable and essential mnemonic for the spiritual progress of the individual towards perfection. It is just such an ideology which Margery Kempe consciously espouses on her own multiple pilgrimages. Whilst making her way through Europe on her journey to the earthly Jerusalem, for example, she is accused by her fellow pilgrims of taking the pilgrimage all too seriously, to which she responds emphatically that God is just as mighty in foreign climates as he is at home, and that he is just as worthy of their love when they are abroad as when they are in their own country (60) Similarly, during the same pilgrimage Margery is ill-treated and humiliated by her fellow pilgrims because she will not share in their hedonistic ribaldry and because she insists on talking of holy matters. There can be little doubt, then, that Margery is engaging directly with the debate surrounding pilgrimage which left the reformist wing of the Church (led by Wycliffe and later taken up by the Lollards) highly critical of the secularisation of pilgrimage and its resultant licentiousness – something also satirised in *The Canterbury Tales*.

One of Margery's primary motives for embarking on her Jerusalem pilgrimage, however, is to receive remission for her sins. Established as a primary means of purchasing remission of the purgatorial sentence following the edict of Pope Celestine V in 1294 (indeed, pilgrimage to the locations of the Passion in Jerusalem purchased full plenary remission of sins for the devout pilgrim),[38] it is evident that by the early fifteenth century pilgrimage had become subject to abuse, and frequently offered the pilgrim the opportunity to indulge in hedonistic practices which would be forbidden within

---

[37] Venetia Nelson (ed.), *A Myrour to Lewde Men and Wymmen: A Prose Version of the 'Speculum Vitae'*, Middle English Texts 14 (Heidelberg, 1981), p. 71 (my translation).

[38] Sumption, *Pilgrimage*, p. 142.

the regulated domestic or ecclesiastic environment at home. In this context, pilgrimages for one particular follower of Wyclif

> seem to be caused by the deceitfulness of the fiend and by his covetous and worldly priests, for such pilgrimages commonly maintain lechery, gluttony, drunkenness, extortions, wrongdoings and worldly vanities.[39]

The reformist view here extemporised focuses not on any symbolic meaning to pilgrimage, but on its degeneration into self-indulgence and hedonistic pleasure. For this author at least – and corroborated by the experiences of Margery Kempe – pilgrimage, like everything else, had become subject to the monetary values of the marketplace and to the shallow materialism which was everywhere apparent in the newly commercialised urban centres from which many of the pilgrims were drawn. As a result, for many of its adherents, pilgrimage had become the nurturer of immorality rather than a means to achieve salvation – something which is made fully apparent in the physical and spiritual threats to which Margery Kempe becomes prey during her own pilgrimages, both at home and abroad, as many of the extracts here translated demonstrate.

Female mysticism and the continental tradition

Besides providing further expression of pious affectivity, Margery's pilgrimages also succeed in increasing her own sense of spiritual authority. It is, for example, highly significant that her reception in Europe, particularly in Italy where she spends some time both preceding and following her trip to Jerusalem, is much more favourable and tolerant than she could later expect whilst travelling around the English countryside. Whereas in England her sojourns are characterised by arrests and accusations and physical intimidation, in Italy she tends to find greater acceptance and accord.[40] Significantly too, this is a response which is frequently instigated by women rather than men, thus serving to augment the sense of a pious and literary female spiritual community, beginning with a variety of female saints, as we have seen, and extending to the women she encounters throughout Europe. One memorable expression of such female soli-

---

[39] Anne Hudson (ed.), *Selections of English Wycliffite Writings* (Cambridge, 1978), pp. 86–7 (my translation).

[40] Sarah Beckwith examines the problems connected with authority within the English mystical tradition in her essay, 'Problems of Authority in Later Medieval English Mysticism: Language, Agency, and Authority in *The Book of Margery Kempe*', *Exemplaria* 4 (1992), pp. 171–200.

darity occurs on the dangerous and bandit-ridden road back to Rome where Margery is overcome by her emotional response to a Christ-like doll being carried by one of her female travelling companions. She tells how, following her collapse, she is taken in and solicitously cared for by a group of women who recognise her sanctity and take pity on her plight (43–4)

On a later occasion, she tells also how the elegantly named Margaret Florentyne, an Italian noblewoman, cares for her generously, feeding her food off her own table and eagerly seeking her spiritual advice (95–6). It is also in Italy that Margery visits the shrine of the recently deceased and canonised Saint Bridget (97–8), a saint whose name and example crop up regularly in Margery's narrative and who evidently played an influential role in Margery's call to the holy life and decision to have her experiences written down.[41] Thus it would appear that, rather than rely entirely for her authority upon the rather patchy English – and male – tradition of mystical writing invoked elsewhere in her book, Margery prefers to look towards the rich continental tradition of female mysticism and female literary production with which to identify.

Unlike the continental experience, there had been a singular absence of documented mystical activity in England from the time of Christina of Markyate in the twelfth century until what has been identified as a 'magnificent flowering' of mystical activity in the fourteenth and fifteenth centuries.[42] The first half of the fourteenth century laid claim to the Yorkshire mystic, Richard Rolle, whose work, as we have seen, had an influence upon Margery's own writing, and the anonymous author of *The Cloud of Unknowing* (not mentioned by Margery). The *Book* also testifies to the popularity of the writing of Walter Hilton whose mystical treatise, *The Scale of Perfection*, is also mentioned as one of the books Margery had read to her by a supportive priest (95). Also exercising an influence upon Margery was Julian of Norwich who was living as a recluse in Norwich at the time of Margery's religious conversion, and with whom Margery spent two days or more discussing her own mystical experiences in 1413 (92–4). Julian probably already had one text in the public domain by this stage[43] (although there is no evidence to suggest that Margery was familiar with it), and Margery takes a great

---

41 See for example, Meech and Allen, *Book*, pp. 39, 47, 143.
42 David Knowles, *The English Mystical Tradition* (London, 1961), p. 46.
43 The only extant copy of Julian's Short Text is dated explicitly by its scribe as 1413.

deal of comfort from her gently supportive advice, telling us that Julian was 'expert in such matters' (that is to say, the mystical experience; 92). Nevertheless, in spite of these influences and perhaps also because of East Anglia's geographical proximity to the continent, it was to Europe – and to Saint Bridget in particular – that Margery turned for her primary inspiration and authority, both as holy woman and as author.

From the tenth century onwards, mainland Europe had borne witness to a long stream of female mystics from Hrotsvitha of Gandersheim and Hildegarde of Bingen, in the tenth and twelfth centuries respectively, to the famous mystics of the convent of Helfta in the late thirteenth century.[44] There is no direct evidence that the writings of these women were readily available to women like Margery, but we do have evidence which suggests that the writing of their spiritual daughters such as Bridget of Sweden and Catherine of Siena, along with the spiritual biographies of other continental female mystics, had entered the English textual community by the time that Margery came to write her own book. In fact, traces of Bridget of Sweden's *Revelations* had begun to appear in English texts by the 1370s, especially those with an East Anglian provenance, and again this is one of the texts which Margery mentions by name as having been read to her by a priest (95). Bridget had been canonised in 1391, and one of the most active supporters of her canonisation had been Cardinal Adam Easton of Norwich. The link between Bridget and East Anglia had been further strengthened by the donation in 1406 of Henry Lord Fitzhugh's estate at Cherry Hinton near Cambridge to the order of Brigittine nuns established after the saint's death in Rome in 1373. This had been followed by the founding of Syon Abbey in London (and its sister-house across the river at Sheen) for the Brigittines by Henry V in 1415. It was this religious house which Margery visited in the 1430s to obtain a pardon, only a few years prior to embarking on the writing of her own mystical text [245].

---

[44] On these women see Katharina M. Wilson (ed.), *Medieval Women Writers* (Manchester, 1984). For a selection of Hrosvitha's writing in translation see Katharina M. Wilson, *Hrotsvit of Gandersheim: A Florilegium of her Works* (Cambridge, 1998); on Hildegarde see Newman, *Sister of Wisdom*, op. cit.; on the Helfta visionaries see M. J. Finnegan, *The Women of Helfta: Scholars and Mystics* (Athens, GA & London, 1991). Examples of the writing of these women in translation along with a useful introduction can be found in Alexandra Barratt, *Women's Writing in Middle English* (London, 1992).

Thus it would seem that the *Revelations* of Saint Bridget in partic-ular had offered Margery the example of a holy woman who had also been a wife and a mother, who had transcended these obstacles and who had found an authoritative voice with which to disseminate her extraordinary religious insights and mystical experiences. Like Margery, Bridget was a woman who had also met with considerable dissent, had successfully countered much ecclesiastic misogyny within a culture of suspicion of the outspoken female, and who had won for herself acceptance, authority and no small measure of autonomy.[45] Thus, when Margery tells us of how in Rome she visits Bridget's handmaid, and kneels in the spot where Saint Bridget had knelt (98), the incident stands as a paradigm within the *Book* for Margery's buying into the type of female authority and textual community which Bridget represented to her and which she was herself to set in place in England with the writing of her book. In effect she both merges with – and significantly outdoes – this author-itative and orthodox precursor and in so doing inaugurates, alongside Julian of Norwich, a rich and highly individual seam of women's writing in English, moving gradually but inexorably from the margins of acceptability into the centre of the English literary canon. It will therefore come as no surprise to her readers that it was on July 23rd 1436, a day dedicated to the honour of the newly canonised Saint Bridget, that Margery Kempe began to instigate the writing of her own inimitable book, bringing to fruitful conclusion the desire to share her own remarkable 'secrets' with the world at large: 'by this book many people shall be turned to (God) and believe in (him)' (103).

The most recent and authoritative study of Saint Bridget to date is Bridget Morris, *St Birgitta of Sweden* (Cambridge, 1999). For a translated edition of the *Revelationes* see Julia Bolton Holloway, *Saint Bride and her Book: Birgitta of Sweden's* Revelations (Cambridge, 1992).

Note on the Translations

The Book of Margery Kempe is essentially a record of an intensely spiritual journey, documented within the context of a lived life and reflecting all its haphazardness, distractions, set-backs and progressions. Lived lives are not ordered and linear in the main; they are chaotic and cyclical, and an attempt is made by the imposition of monolithic ideologies upon them to create some sense of order and purpose within them. This abridged translation of *The Book of Margery Kempe*, then, is comprised of passages selected from the spiritual journey of its author, and in many ways the choice of material echoes its schematic haphazardness as well as its arresting moments of order and culmination. Like the *Book* itself, therefore, it 'is not written in order, everything after another as it happened' (103), but is rearranged thematically, each passage informing the next and entering into dialogue with the other extracts included within the same section. Where necessary, translated episodes have been contextualised in order to get some sense of where they fit into the chronology of the whole, but each episode can either be read alone or else as comprising part of an ongoing discourse within the *Book*. In other words, each extract can be taken autonomously, or else pieced together within the jigsaw which is *The Book of Margery Kempe*, and assert itself as part of the integrity of the entire text.

The episodes here selected for translation have been separated into three thematic strands – strands which I consider to be fundamental to the hermeneutic structure of the *Book* – that is to say its primary means of explanation. They are also representative of the ways in which Margery Kempe makes use of specifically feminine discourses as a means of explicating her own experiences and of imbuing them with a measure of authority. Whereas these three thematic strands are ubiquitous throughout the *Book*, they also rise rhythmically to the surface and assert their own discursive pre-eminence at regular intervals, before ceding to other insistent discourses within the text.

The three primary discourses which I have chosen to prioritise are those of motherhood, sexuality, and voice. Of these three, it is motherhood which forms the most powerful matrix within this text, being fundamental to a subjectivity which Margery successfully rewrites in order to achieve her desired goal of perfection. Similarly, her use of a variety of discourses of female sexuality as a means of achieving authority is equally as insistent, as indeed is her defiant stance against those cultural narratives which have served to vilify – and silence – the female voice. In effect, by means of her re-appropriation of these discourses, Margery Kempe succeeds in transforming both female body and its dangerous voice into the authoritative site from which God speaks.

This translation retains Margery Kempe's use of the third-person perspective within the text, in spite of its potentially archaic and mystifying effect. The primary reason for this is in order to preserve some sense of its importance as a distancing tool within the original text; whilst using the female body, and specifically her *own* body to create authority and to explicate her experiences, Margery Kempe also illustrates an express desire to make her writing of universal relevance. The use of the third-person as an objectifying agent within the narrative, echoing as it does the formulaic approaches of male-authored traditional hagiography, serves to imbue the writing with additional *gravitas* and authority because of its invocation of established generic – and gendered – convention. Another consideration, of course, was the ubiquitous threat posed to the writer by accusations of heresy which everywhere lurk as a sub-text. It is pertinent here to recall that Margery's early fourteenth-century Parisian precursor, Margeurite Porete, went to the stake and was burned along with her book. Margery's preference for the use of the third person therefore serves to act as a shield behind which she is able to operate, whilst at the same time offering both author and text some protection from labels of heterodoxy.

In rendering selections of the *Book* into modern English, I have attempted to retain much of the linguistic cadence and rhythm of the original Middle English, reflecting as they do the intensely *oral* nature of this text. For this reason, the long sentence structure of the original, and the repetitive use of the conjunction 'and' have also both been retained in the main, except where the convolutedness of sentences would considerably impair understanding – although punctuation has been modified and increased in order to accommodate modern sensibilities. The decision to retain the characteristic verboseness of the original text will also serve to preserve a proximity to the author's own voice which would otherwise be lost. The *Book* is offered to us as the direct product of Margery Kempe's words spilling forth from her own mouth and taking shape – albeit with the help of the scribe – upon the page. To edit out this immediacy of a life told 'according to her own tongue' [221] would therefore be to destroy the living vibrancy of what remains a uniquely oral text.

Finally, I do not intend to defend the choice of material included here against charges of subjectiveness. Quite simply, these extracts narrate those episodes which I consider best render Margery Kempe the idiosyncratic – and remarkable – person she remains, reflecting both her intense charisma, her endearing vulnerability, and her some-times infuriating self-obsession; most of all they reflect her flawed humanity and her sense of superior purpose. What I hope the reader will be left with at the end of this book is a sense of Margery as both an ordinary and extraordinary woman struggling to make her mark on an antipathetic, masculine world, and attempting against enor-mous odds to make a difference. Moreover, Margery's struggle to come to writing has allowed us a glimpse of a most unusual visionary. Indeed, her account of her own remarkable experiences has opened up for her modern audience a far deeper insight into late medieval female spirituality, and the variety of subject positions available for women within the up-and-coming mercantile milieu of late-medieval England, than would otherwise have been available.

The Book of Margery Kempe

I. Narratives of Motherhood

The Birth of Margery's First Child [*Book*, pp. 6–9]

When this creature was aged twenty or a little more, she was married to a respected burgess and within a short time she became pregnant, as nature would have it. And following this conception she was troubled by severe attacks of illness until the child was born, and then, what with the efforts of childbirth and the preceding sickness, she despaired of her life, believing she would die. At that point she summoned her confessor, for she retained in her conscience something which she had never revealed before that time in all her life. For she was always prevented by her enemy, the devil, who continually told her whilst she was in good health that she had no need of confession but to do penance entirely on her own, and all should be forgiven, for God is merciful enough. And so this creature often did great penance in fasting on bread and water and undertook other charitable deeds with devout prayers, except she would not reveal that sin in confession. And when she was at any time sick or troubled, the devil said in her mind that she should be damned for she was not shriven of that fault.

For this reason, after the birth of her child and not expecting to live, she sent for her confessor, as mentioned before, fully intending to be absolved of a lifetime of sins, as near as she could. And when she came to the point of uttering that thing which she had concealed for so long, her confessor was a little too hasty and began to reprimand her sharply before she had fully said what she intended to, and so she would say nothing more, for anything he might do. And soon afterwards, on account of the fear she had of damnation on the one hand, and his sharp reproving on the other, this creature went out of her mind and was amazingly tormented and troubled with spirits for half a year, eight weeks and odd days.

And during this time she thought she saw devils opening their mouths which were all alight with burning flames of fire, as if they would have swallowed her in; sometimes they pawed at her, sometimes threatening her, sometimes pulling at her and dragging her about both night and day during the said time. And the devils also called out to her with great threats and exhorted her to forsake her

Christian faith and to deny her God, his mother and all the saints in heaven, her good works and all good virtues, her father, her mother, and all her friends. And so she did. She slandered her husband, her friends and her own self; she spoke many a vituperative and sharp word; she knew neither virtue nor goodness; she desired all wickedness. Just as the spirits tempted her to say and do, so she said and did. She would have killed herself many a time as they incited her to do and would have been damned with them in hell, in witness of which she bit her own hand so violently that it was evident all her life thereafter. And she also pitilessly tore the skin on her body over her heart with her fingernails, for she had no other implements, and she would have done something worse except she was bound up and restrained with force both day and night so that she could not do as she wanted.

And when she had been long troubled by these and many other temptations, so that people believed that she would never escape with her life, then one time as she lay alone and her keepers were away from her, our merciful Lord Christ Jesus who is ever to be trusted – worshipped be his name who never forsakes his servant in time of need – appeared to his creature who had forsaken him. He appeared in the likeness of a man, the most seemly, most beauteous and most amiable that could ever be seen with a person's eye, clad in a mantle of purple silk and sitting upon the side of her bed, gazing upon her with so blessed a countenance that she was strengthened in all her spirits, and he spoke these words to her: 'Daughter, why have you forsaken me when I never forsook you?' And as soon as he had said these words, truly she saw the air open up as bright as any flash of lightning, and he ascended into the air, not hastily and quickly, but beautifully and gradually, so that she was able to behold him clearly in the air until it closed again.

And soon the creature grew stable in her wits and reason as ever she had been before, and as soon as her husband came to her she entreated him to let her have the keys of the larder to fetch her food and drink as she had done previously. Her maids and her keepers advised him that he should not deliver any keys to her, for they said she would only give away such goods as there were, for they considered she did not know what she was saying. Nevertheless, her husband, who always had tenderness and compassion for her, commanded that they should hand over the keys to her. And she took her food and drink as her bodily strength would allow her, and she recognised again her friends and household and all the other people who came to her to witness how our Lord Jesus Christ had worked his grace in her – so, blessed may he be who is ever near us in our tribulation, for, when people believe he is absent from them, he is very near through his grace. After that, this creature performed all her responsibilities wisely and soberly enough, except that she did not truly understand the spiritual call[1] of our Lord.

The Conception of Margery's Last Child [*Book*, pp. 48–50]

Margery's fourteenth and last child is born in 1413, probably sometime during March – and three months or so before Margery manages to forge a vow of chastity with her husband on Midsummer's Eve. This would mean that the child is about six months old when Margery embarks upon her pilgrimage to Jerusalem sometime in the autumn of 1413.[2]

During the time when this creature had revelations, our Lord said to her, 'Daughter, you are pregnant.'

She replied, 'Ah, Lord, what am I going to do then about caring for my child?'

Our Lord said, 'Daughter, don't be afraid, I shall arrange for it to be cared for.'

'Lord, I am not worthy to hear you speak and continue to have sex with my husband in this way, in spite of its being a source of great pain and distress to me.'

'For that reason it is no sin for you, daughter; rather it is reward and merit; and you will not have any the less grace, for I want you to bring forth more fruit for me.'

Then the creature said, 'Lord Jesus, this way of life belongs to your holy virgins.'

'Yes, daughter, but be very well assured that I also love wives, and especially those wives who would live chaste, if they might have their will, and do their duty to please me as you do.[3] For, though the state of virginity be more perfect and more holy than the state of

---

1   The Middle English term used here is 'drawt', a word which, when used by Margery, is frequently imbued with connotations of spiritual ecstasy or rapture. She uses the term consistently in the *Book* to describe the ability of God to draw his lovers to him.

2   There has been some debate about the chronology of the birth of Margery's last child. For a more detailed appraisal of the evidence see my article, 'Margery's Last Child: A Refutation', *Notes and Queries* n.s. 46, 2 (June 1999), pp. 181–3.

3   As well as drawing on patristic debate as to whether virgins were dearer to Christ than married women, Margery is probably also being informed by the current popularity of the maternal saint, Elizabeth of Hungary. This maternal saint is specifically named elsewhere in the *Book* and her piety was also characterised by loud crying.

widowhood, and the state of widowhood more perfect than the state of marriage, yet, daughter, I love you as well as any virgin in the world. Nobody may prevent me from loving whomsoever I wish and as much as I wish, for love, daughter, quenches all sin. And therefore ask of me the gifts of love. There is no gift as holy as the gift of love, nor is anything to be so much desired as love, for love may purchase whatever it desires. And for this reason, daughter, you may please God no better than to continually contemplate his love.'

Then this creature asked our Lord Jesus how she should best love him. And our Lord said, 'Be mindful of your wickedness and think about my goodness.'

She replied, 'I am the most unworthy creature that ever you showed grace to on earth.'

'Ah, daughter, 'said our Lord, 'do not be afraid. I take no account what a person has been, but I take heed of what he will be. Daughter, you have despised yourself, for which reason you shall never be despised by God. Bear in mind, daughter, what Mary Magdalene was, Mary the Egyptian, Saint Paul, and many other saints who are now in heaven, for the unworthy I make worthy, and the sinful I make righteous.[4] And so have I made you worthy to me, once loved and evermore loved by me. There is no saint in heaven with whom you would wish to speak, who will not come to you. Whomsoever God loves, the saints love too. When you please God, you please his mother and all the saints in heaven. Daughter, I take witness of my mother, of all the angels in heaven, and of all the saints in heaven that I love you with all my heart and I may not do without your love.'

Our Lord then said to his blessed mother, 'Blessed Mother, tell my daughter of the greatness of the love I bear for her.'

Then this creature lay still, weeping and sobbing as if her heart would break for the sweetness of our Lord's words which he spoke to her soul. Immediately afterwards, the Queen of Mercy, God's mother, communed[5] with the soul of this creature, saying, 'My

---

4   These saints were all renowned for their former concupiscence, later becoming symbolic of the redeemed sexual sinner. It is likely that, given Margery's married and maternal status, she is drawing upon these orthodox figures here to lend support to her call to the holy life.

5   The Middle English word here is 'dalyed'. I have chosen not to use the more usual translation of 'conversed', however, since it does not convey the mystical (and indeed, erotic) overtones which are everywhere apparent in Margery's employment of the term. Instead, I have attempted here and elsewhere to imbue the translation with the sense of 'union'.

beloved daughter, I bring you sure tidings, bearing witness for my sweet son Jesus with all angels and all saints in heaven who love you most highly. Daughter, I am your mother, your lady and your mistress, to teach you in every way how you shall best please God.' She taught this creature and informed her so wonderfully that she was embarrassed to speak of it or tell it to anyone, the matters were so elevated and so holy, except to the anchorite who was her principal confessor,[6] for he was most knowledgeable in such things. And he ordered this creature by virtue of obedience to tell him whatever she felt, and so she did.

Imitatio Mariae at Jerusalem [*Book*, pp. 66–75]

During her pilgrimage to Jerusalem, Margery finds herself very unpopular with her fellow pilgrims who frequently abandon her or treat her harshly because of what they regard as her excessive piety. It is during this pilgrimage, however, that Margery first experiences the 'gift of tears' which will characterise her religiosity ever afterwards.

[T]his company which had excluded the said creature from their table so that she should no longer eat amongst them, organized a ship for themselves to sail in. They bought vessels for their wine and arranged bedding for themselves, but nothing for her. Seeing their unkindness, she then went to the same man whom they had been to and provided herself with bedding as they had done, and came to where they were and showed them what she had done, intending to sail with them in that ship which they had arranged.

Afterwards, as this creature was in contemplation, our Lord warned her in her mind not to sail in that ship and he assigned her another ship, a galley,[7] that she should sail in. Then she told this to some of the company who relayed it to their friends, and then they did not dare to sail in the ship which they had organized. And so they sold off the vessels which they had bought for their wine and were very glad to come to the galley where she was; and so, although it was against their will, she went on with them in their company, for they did not dare do otherwise.

---

6 This reference is to the anchorite attached to the Dominican Friary of Bishop's Lynn who preceded Richard Spryngolde as Margery's principal confessor.
7 A small pilgrim boat which would have been privately owned and profit driven. It would probably have undertaken an annual trip to the Holy Land from Venice and back again loaded with pilgrims.

When it was time to make up their beds, they locked up her bed-clothes, and a priest who was in their company took away a sheet from the said creature and said it was his. She took God to witness that it was her sheet. Then the priest swore a great oath by the book in his hand that she was as false as could be and he despised her, and severely rebuked her.

And so continually she had much tribulation until she arrived in Jerusalem. And before she arrived, she said to them that she supposed that they were aggrieved with her:

'I pray you, sirs, be in charity with me, for I am in charity with you, and forgive me that I have annoyed you along the way. And if any of you has trespassed against me in any way, God forgive you for it, just as I do.'

And so they went on into the Holy Land until they could see Jerusalem. And when this creature – she was riding on an ass – saw Jerusalem, she thanked God with all her heart, praying him for his mercy that, just as he had brought her to see his earthly city Jerusalem, so he would grant her grace to see the blissful city of Jerusalem above, the city of heaven. Answering her thought, our Lord Jesus Christ granted her her desire. Then, for joy that she had and the sweetness that she felt in her communing with our Lord, she was on the point of falling off her ass, for she could not bear the sweetness and grace that God wrought in her soul. Then, two German pilgrims, one of whom was a priest, went up to her and kept her from falling off, and he put spices in her mouth to comfort her, thinking she was ill. In this way they helped her onwards to Jerusalem. And when she arrived there she said, 'Sirs, I pray you not to be displeased though I weep bitterly in this holy place where our Lord Jesus Christ lived and died.'

Then they went to the Church of the Holy Sepulchre in Jerusalem,[8] and they were let in on the one day at evensong and remained inside until the next day at evensong time. Then the friars lifted up a cross and led the pilgrims about from one place to another where our Lord had suffered his pains and his Passion, every man and woman bearing a wax candle in one hand. As they moved about, the friars continually told them what our Lord suffered in every place. And the said creature wept and sobbed as copiously as if she had seen our Lord suffering his Passion at that time with her bodily eyes. She saw him truly before her in her soul by means of contemplation, and that

---

[8]   This church was built on the supposed location of Christ's Passion, Mount Calvary being signified by a rocky elevation within the church itself.

caused her to have compassion. And when they came up onto Mount Calvary, she fell down so that she could neither stand nor kneel, but writhed and twisted with her body, spreading her arms out wide, and she cried with a loud voice as though her heart would burst apart, for in the city of her soul she saw truly and freshly how our Lord was crucified. Before her face she heard and saw in her spiritual sight the mourning of our Lady, of Saint John and Mary Magdalene and many others who loved our Lord.

And she had such great compassion and such great pain to see our Lord's pain that she was not able to keep herself from crying and roaring though she should have died for it. And this was the first crying that she ever cried in any contemplation, and this manner of crying lasted many years after this time for anything that anybody might do, and she suffered much malice and much reproof for it. The crying was so loud and so amazing that it made the people astonished, unless they had heard it before or else they knew the reason for the crying, and she experienced it so many times that it made her very weak in her bodily strength, and particularly if she heard of our Lord's Passion. And sometimes when she saw the crucifix, or if she saw a man or animal had a wound, whichever it were, or if a man beat a child in front of her or whipped a horse or any other animal, if she were to see or hear it, she thought she saw our Lord being beaten or wounded, just as she witnessed it in the man or in the animal, either in the fields or the town, or when she was on her own as well as amongst the people.

When she had her cryings first at Jerusalem, she experienced them frequently, as she did in Rome also. And when she returned home to England, on her arrival the cryings only happened seldom at first, once a month as it were. Afterwards they happened once a week, then daily. Once she had fourteen in one day; and another day she had seven, and so as God would visit her with them, sometimes in church, sometimes in the street, sometimes in her chamber, sometimes in the field when God would send them, for she never knew the time nor the hour when they would come. And they never came without very great sweetness of devotion and high contemplation. And as soon as she perceived that she was going to cry she would keep it in as much as she could so that people should not hear it and become annoyed. For some said it was a wicked spirit that vexed her; some said it was an illness; some said she had drunk too much wine; some cursed her; some wished she was in the harbour; some wished her in a bottomless boat; and so said each person as he thought. Other spiritual people loved her and favoured her all the more. Some great clerks claimed that our Lady never cried as much nor any saint in heaven, but they knew very little of what she felt, nor would they believe that she was unable to refrain from crying if she had wanted to.

And therefore, when she knew that she was about to cry, she kept it in as long as she could and did all that she could to withstand it, or else to put it away until she turned as ashen as lead, and constantly it would seethe increasingly in her mind, until that time when it burst out. And when her body could no longer endure the spiritual exertion but was overcome with the unspeakable love which worked so fervently in her soul, then she fell down and cried amazingly loud. And the more she struggled to keep it in or to suppress it, so much the more would she cry, and even louder.

And this is what happened on Mount Calvary, as previously written. She had as true a contemplation in the sight of her soul as if Christ had been hanging before her bodily eye in his manhood. And when, through dispensation of the high mercy of our Sovereign Saviour Jesus Christ, it was granted this creature to see so vividly his precious tender body hanging upon the cross, completely rent and torn with scourges, more full of wounds than ever a dovecote was of holes,[9] with the crown of thorns upon his head, his blissful hands, his tender feet nailed to the hard wood, the rivers of blood flowing out plenteously from every limb, the grisly and grievous wound in his precious side shedding blood and water for her love and her salvation, then she fell down and cried out with a loud voice, writhing and twisting her body amazingly from side to side, spreading her arms asunder as if she would have died. Nor could she prevent herself from crying, nor control these bodily contortions, because of the fire of love that burnt so fervently in her soul with pure pity and compassion.

It is not to be wondered at if this creature cried and made astonishing facial expressions when we may see every day with our own eyes both men and women – some for loss of worldly goods, some for affection of their kin or for worldly friendships, through excessive

---

[9] This is an image which also appears in Richard Rolle's *Meditations on the Passion* ('Sweet Jesus, your body is like a dove-cot. For a dove-cot is full of holes . . .'), for which see *English Writings of Richard Rolle of Hampole*, ed. Hope Emily Allen (Oxford, 1931), p. 35 (my translation). In turn, it is likely that Rolle is reliant, at least in part, on the image found in the Song of Songs 2: 14 ('My dove in the clefts of the rock, in the hollow places of the wall, shew me thy face, let thy voice sound in my ears: for thy voice is sweet, and thy face comely').

study and earthly affection, and most of all for inordinate love and physical affection if their friends are parted from them – who will cry out, roar and wring their hands as if they were witless and mindless, and yet they know well enough that they displease God. And if anyone advises them to leave off and cease their weeping or crying, they will say that they are unable to; they loved their friend so much and he was so gentle and so kind to them they may in no way forget him. How much more might they weep, cry and roar if their most beloved friend were seized violently before their eyes and brought before the judge with all manner of reproof, and wrongfully condemned to death – and especially so shameful a death as our merciful Lord suffered for our sake. How should they endure it? Without doubt they would both cry and roar and avenge themselves if they might, or else people would say they were no friends. Alas, alas for sorrow, that the death of a creature who has often sinned and trespassed against his Maker should be so immeasurably mourned and sorrowed for. And it is an offence against God and an impediment to souls on either side. And the compassionate death of our Saviour, by which we are all restored to life, is not borne in mind by us unworthy and unkind wretches, nor will we support our Lord's confidantes whom he has clothed with love, but rather disparage them and hinder them as much as we may.

When this creature, along with her company, reached the grave where our Lord was buried, as she entered that holy place she fell down with her candle in her hand as if she would have died for sorrow. And afterwards she rose up again with great weeping and sobbing as though she had seen our Lord buried right in front of her. Then she thought she saw our Lady in her soul, how she mourned and wept for her son's death; and then was our Lady's sorrow her own sorrow.

And so wherever the friars led them in that holy place, she always wept and sobbed amazingly, and especially when she came to where our Lord was nailed on the cross. There she cried and wept without control so that she was unable to restrain herself. Also, they came to a marble slab upon which our Lord was laid when he was taken down from the cross, and there she wept with great compassion, being mindful of our Lord's Passion.

Afterwards, she received communion on Mount Calvary and then she wept, she sobbed, she cried so loudly that it was amazing to hear it. She was so full of holy thoughts and meditations and holy contemplations on the Passion of our Lord Jesus Christ, and holy conversation in which our Lord communed with her soul, that she was never able to express them afterwards, so elevated and holy were they. Much was the grace that our Lord showed to this creature while she was three weeks in Jerusalem.

Another day early in the morning they visited the great hills, and her guides told where our Lord bore the cross on his back and where his mother met with him, and how she fainted, and how she fell down and he fell down also. And so they travelled on all the morning until they came to Mount Zion, and all the way this creature wept copiously for compassion of our Lord's Passion. On Mount Zion is a place where our Lord washed his disciples' feet, and a little way off from there he celebrated the Last Supper with his disciples.

And for this reason this creature had great desire to receive communion in that holy place where our merciful Lord Jesus Christ first consecrated his precious body in the form of bread and gave it to his disciples. And so she experienced great devotion, with plenteous tears and with boisterous sobbings, for in this place there is plenary remission, as is there also in four other places in the Church of the Holy Sepulchre. One is on Mount Calvary; another at the grave where our Lord was buried; the third is at the marble slab on which his precious body was laid when it was taken down from the cross; the fourth is where the holy cross was buried; and in many other places in Jerusalem.

And, when this creature came to the place where the apostles received the Holy Ghost, our Lord gave her great devotion. Afterwards she went to the place where our Lady was buried and as she knelt on her knees during the hearing of two masses, our Lord Jesus Christ said to her, 'You do not come here out of any necessity, daughter, but for merit and reward, for your sins were forgiven you before you came here, and you therefore came here only to increase your reward and your merit. And I am well pleased with you, daughter, for you remain obedient to Holy Church and because you obey your confessor and follow his advice, who by the authority of Holy Church has absolved you of your sins and has dispensed you, so that you need not go to Rome or Saint James at Compostela unless you yourself so desire.[10] Notwithstanding all this, I command you in the name of Jesus, daughter, that you go to visit these holy places and do as I bid you, for I am above Holy Church and I shall go with you and look after you very well.'

---

[10] Margery visited the popular pilgrim destination of Santiago de Compostela in northern Spain, probably in July 1417.

Then our Lady spoke to her soul in this manner, saying, 'Daughter, you are well blessed, for my son Jesus shall suffuse you with so much grace that all the world shall wonder at you. Do not be ashamed, my dear daughter, to receive the gifts which my son shall give you, for I tell you truly they will be great gifts that he will give you. And therefore, my dear daughter, do not be ashamed of him who is your God, your Lord and your love, any more than I was to cry and to weep for the pain of my sweet son, Jesus Christ, when I saw him hanging on the cross; nor was Mary Magdalene ashamed to cry and weep for my son's love. And therefore, daughter, if you wish to partake in our joy, you must partake in our sorrow.'

This creature experienced these sweet words and communing at our Lady's grave, and much more than she could ever describe.

And afterwards she went to Bethany where Mary and Martha dwelt, and to the grave where Lazarus was buried and raised from the dead back to life. And she was also in the chapel where our blessed Lord appeared to his blissful mother before all others on the morning of Easter Day.[11] And she stood in the same place where Mary Magdalene stood when Christ said to her, 'Mary, why are you weeping?' And so she was in many more places than can be written, for she was three weeks in Jerusalem and the surrounding country.

The Devotional Doll [*Book*, pp. 75–8]

Abandoned by her fellow pilgrims on the way back to Rome from Jerusalem, Margery finds unexpected fellowship along the way.

And then our Lord commanded her to go to Rome and from there home to England, saying to her, 'Daughter, as often as you say or think, "Worshipped be all those holy places in Jerusalem in which Christ suffered bitter pain and passion", you shall have the same pardon as if you were there bodily, both for yourself and for all those to whom you will give it.'[12]

---

11 The Chapel of the Apparition, dating from the fourteenth century and situated in the Church of the Holy Sepulchre. Margery's vision of Christ appearing to his mother on Easter morning here echoes a widespread tradition of the Middle Ages, in spite of the fact that Mark 16: 9 states that it was to Mary Magdalene that Christ made his first appearance.

12 As Margery has already pointed out, several of the sites at Jerusalem offered plenary indulgence – that is remission of all sins – for those pilgrims who visited them. It would seem here that Margery is being offered the same remission for mere meditation on these sites, exonerating her from having to make the journey again. However, in fact she has already been granted forgiveness for all her sins

And as she journeyed towards Venice, many of her companions fell very ill and all the time our Lord said to her, 'Don't be afraid, daughter, nobody will die in the ship that you are in.' And she found that her feelings were completely true. And, when our Lord had delivered them to Venice again in safety, her countrymen forsook her and went away from her, leaving her alone. And some of them said that they would not go with her for a hundred pounds.

And when they had gone away from her, then our Lord Jesus Christ, who always helps in need and never forsakes his servant who truly trusts to his mercy, said to this creature, 'Do not be afraid, daughter, for I shall ordain for you very well and bring you safely to Rome and home again to England without any shame to your body, if you will dress yourself in white clothes and wear them as I instructed you whilst you were in England.'[13]

Then this creature, feeling great heaviness and great perplexity, answered again in her mind, 'If you are the spirit of God who speaks in my soul and I may prove you to be a true spirit through the Church's counsel, I shall obey your will; and, if you bring me to Rome in safety, I shall wear white clothes for your love, though all the world should wonder at me.'

'Go forth, daughter, in the name of Jesus, for I am the spirit of God who shall help you in all your need, go with you, and support you in every place, and therefore do not mistrust me. You never found me deceiving, nor do I bid you to do anything but that which is of worship to God and profit to your soul if you will obey, and I shall suffuse you with a great abundance of grace.'

Just then, as she looked to one side, she saw a poor man sitting down who had a great hump on his back. His clothes were all completely ragged, and he seemed a man of about fifty years of age. Then she went to him and said, 'Good man, what is wrong with your back?'

---

in perpetuity by Christ during a vision in Chapter 5, pointing towards a persistent anxiety about her own sinfulness which characterises the *Book*, and particularly her earlier narratives.

13 White clothing was usually adopted as a symbol of virtue and virginity. In Margery's case she probably adopts it as a sign that she has been bestowed the role of 'virgin in her soul' by Christ (see p. 69). Whilst on pilgrimage, however, she relinquishes her white clothing on a number of occasions, primarily because of the accusations of hypocrisy leveled against her. In response to the bargain struck here with Christ, however, Margery will re-adopt white clothing – this time permanently – following her mystical marriage to the Godhead which takes place when she reaches Rome (see pp. 71–2).

He said, 'It was broken in an illness, mistress.'

She asked what his name was and where he came from. He said his name was Richard and that he came from Ireland. Then she recalled the words of her confessor who was a holy anchorite, as is previously written, who spoke to her whilst she was in England in this way: 'Daughter, when your own companions have forsaken you, God will arrange for a man with a broken back to lead you where you have to go.'

Then, with a glad spirit she said to him, 'Good Richard, lead me to Rome and you shall be rewarded for your effort.'

'No, miss,' he said, 'I know very well that your countrymen have abandoned you and it would therefore be difficult for me to escort you. For your countrymen have both bows and arrows with which to defend both you and themselves, and I have no weapon except a cloak full of patches. And yet I fear that my enemies will rob me and perhaps take you away from me and rape you, and therefore I dare not accompany you, for I would not have you endure any shame in my company for a hundred pounds.'

And then she replied, 'Richard, don't be afraid; God will protect us both very well, and I shall give you two nobles[14] for your effort.'

Then he agreed and set off with her. Soon afterwards there came two Grey Friars and a woman who had come with them from Jerusalem, and she had with her an ass carrying a chest containing an image of our Lord.[15] And then Richard said to the said creature, 'You shall go along with these two men and the woman and I shall meet you morning and evening, for I must go about my search for alms and beg my living.'

And so she followed his advice and travelled on with the friars and the woman. And none of them could understand her language, and yet they provided for her each day food, drink and lodgings as well as they did for themselves and rather better, so that she was always obliged to pray for them. And every evening and morning, Richard with the broken back came and comforted her as he had promised.

And the woman who had the doll in the chest, when they arrived in fine cities, took the doll out of the chest and laid it in the laps of respectable wives. And they would dress it in shirts and kiss it as if it were God himself. And when the creature saw the worship and rever-

---

14 A gold coin in use in England during this period. At this point during the fifteenth century a noble was equivalent to six shillings and eight pence (34p).

15 This 'image of our Lord' would have been a type of devotional doll devised to encourage affective responses.

ence which they bestowed on the doll, she was seized with sweet devotion and sweet meditations, so that she wept with great sobbing and loud crying. And she was moved all the more because whilst in England she had had high meditations on the birth and childhood of Christ, and she thanked God because she saw these creatures had as great a faith in what she saw with her bodily eye as she had witnessed before with her spiritual sight.

When these good women saw this creature weeping, sobbing and crying so amazingly and powerfully so that she was almost overcome by it, then they arranged a good soft bed and laid her upon it, and comforted her as much as they could for our Lord's love – blessed may he be.

Vision of the Nativity [*Book*, pp. 18–20]
Margery's mystical encounters frequently involve visions of key biblical events, in particular the events surrounding the Nativity of Christ and his Passion.

Another day this creature relinquished herself to meditation as she had been commanded before, and she lay still not knowing what she might best think. Then she said to our Lord Jesus Christ, 'Jesus, what shall I think about?'

Our Lord Jesus answered in her mind, 'Daughter, think about my mother, for she is the cause of all the grace that you have.' And then at once she saw Saint Anne,[16] heavily pregnant, and then she prayed Saint Anne to let her be her maid and her servant. And presently our Lady was born, and then she busied herself to take the child to herself and looked after her until she was twelve years old with good food and drink, with fair white clothing and white headscarves. And then she said to the blessed child, 'Lady, you shall be the mother of God.'

The blessed child answered and said, 'I wish I were worthy to be the handmaiden of her who should conceive the Son of God.'

The creature said, 'I pray you, Lady, if that grace befall you, do not discontinue with my service.'

The blessed child disappeared for a certain time, the creature still being in contemplation, and afterwards came back again and said,

---

16 Saint Anne, mother of the Virgin, was also subject to cult status in the later Middle Ages. For an examination of pro-motherhood elements in her cult see Pamela Sheingorn (ed.), *Interpreting Cultural Symbols: Saint Anne in Late Medieval Society* (Athens, GA, 1990).

'Daughter, now I have become the mother of God,' and then the creature fell down on her knees with great reverence and great weeping and said, 'I am not worthy, Lady, to do you service.'

'Yes, daughter,' she said, 'follow me. Your service pleases me well.'

Then she went on with our Lady and with Joseph, carrying with her a bottle of wine containing honey and spices. Then they journeyed to Elizabeth, Saint John the Baptist's mother, and when they met together each of them honoured the other, and so they stayed together with great grace and gladness for twelve weeks. And then Saint John was born, and our Lady picked him up from the ground with great reverence and handed him to his mother, saying of him that he would be a holy man, and blessed him.

Afterwards they took their leave of one another with compassionate tears. And then the creature fell down on her knees to Saint Elizabeth and implored her to pray for her to our Lady so that she might serve her and please her.

'It seems to me, daughter,' said Elizabeth, 'you do your duty very well.'

And then the creature went forth with our Lady to Bethlehem and procured lodgings for her every night with great reverence, and our lady was received with good cheer. Also, she begged for our Lady fair white linen and cloths in which to swaddle her son when he was born; and when Jesus was born, she arranged bedding for our Lady to lie in with her blessed son. And later she begged food for our Lady and her blessed child. Afterwards she swaddled him, weeping bitter tears of compassion, being mindful of the painful death that he would suffer for the love of sinful humanity, saying to him, 'Lord, I shall treat you kindly; I will not bind you too tightly. I pray you, do not be displeased with me.'

And afterwards on the twelfth day, when three kings came with their gifts and worshipped our Lord Jesus Christ who was lying in his mother's lap, this creature, our Lady's handmaiden, beholding the whole process in contemplation, wept amazingly bitterly. And when she saw that they wished to take their leave to go home again into their own countries, she could not bear that they should go from the presence of our Lord, and she cried amazingly sorely that they wanted to go away.

And soon afterwards there came an angel who bade our Lady and Joseph to go from the country of Bethlehem into Egypt. Then this creature went forth with our Lady, day by day procuring her lodgings with great reverence, with many sweet thoughts and high meditations, and high contemplation also, sometimes continuing weeping for two hours and often longer without ceasing in mind of our Lord's Passion. Sometimes she wept for her own sin, sometimes for the sin of the people, sometimes for the souls in purgatory, sometimes for those in poverty or in any distress, for she desired to comfort them all.

Vision of the Passion [*Book*, pp. 187–91]

Then in the sight of her soul she saw our blessed Lord Jesus Christ coming towards his Passion, and before he went, he knelt down and took his mother's blessing. Then she saw his mother falling down in a faint before her son, saying to him, 'Alas, my dear son, how shall I suffer this sorrow and have no joy in all this world but you alone? Ah, dear son, if you must die in any case, let me die before you and let me never suffer this day of sorrow, for I may never bear this sorrow that I shall have for your death. I wish, son, that I might suffer death for you so that you should not die, if mankind might so be saved. Now, dear son, if you have no pity on yourself, have pity on your mother, for you know very well that there is nobody in all this world who can comfort me but you alone.'

Then our Lord took up his mother in his arms and kissed her very sweetly and said to her, 'Ah, blessed mother, be well cheered and comforted, for I have very often told you that I must needs suffer death or else nobody would be saved nor ever enter into bliss. And mother, it is my father's will that it be so, and therefore I pray you let it also be your will, for my death will turn me to great worship and you and all mankind to great joy and profit whoever trusts in my Passion and follows its example. And therefore, blessed mother, you must live here after me, for in you will rest all the faith of Holy Church, and by your faith shall Holy Church increase in her faith. And therefore, I pray you, my beloved mother, cease your sorrowing, for I shall not leave you without comfort. I shall leave with you John, my cousin, to comfort you instead of me; I shall send my holy angels to comfort you on earth; and I shall comfort you in your soul my own self, for mother, you know very well that I have promised you the bliss of heaven, and of that you may be sure. Ah, beloved mother, what would you wish for better than that I should be king and you queen, and that all angels and saints be obedient to your will? And whatever grace you ask of me, I shall not deny your desire. I shall give you power over the devils so that they shall be afraid of you and not you of them. And also, my blessed mother, I have said to you before that when you pass out of this world I shall come for you myself with all my angels and all my saints who are in heaven, and bring you before my father with all manner of music, melody and joy. And I shall set you there in great peace and rest without end. And there you will be crowned Queen of Heaven, Lady of the World, and Empress of Hell. And therefore, my beloved mother, I pray you, bless me and let me go to do my father's will, for that is why I came into this world and took on your flesh and blood.'

When the said creature saw this glorious sight in her soul and saw how he blessed his mother and his mother him, and then how his blessed mother could not speak a single word more to him but fell down to the ground, and how they parted from each other, his mother lying still as if she were dead, then the said creature thought she took our Lord Jesus Christ by the clothes and fell down at his feet, praying him to bless her. And with that she cried very loudly and wept very bitterly saying in her mind, 'Ah, Lord, what shall become of me? I would much rather that you would slay me than let me remain here without you, Lord.'

Then our Lord answered her, 'Be still, daughter, and stay here with my mother and take comfort in her, for she who is my own mother must suffer this sorrow. But I shall come again to my mother, daughter, and comfort both her and you, and turn all your sorrow into joy.'

And then she thought our Lord went forth on his way, and she went to our Lady and said, 'Ah, blessed Lady, rise up and let us follow your blessed son as long as we may see him, so that I may look on him enough before he dies. Ah, dear Lady, how may your heart survive and see your blessed son in all this woe? Lady, I may not endure it, and yet I am not his mother.'

Then our Lady answered and said, 'Daughter, you have heard clearly that it will not be otherwise, and therefore I have to suffer it for my son's love.'

And then she thought that they followed on after our Lord and saw how he said his prayers to his father on the Mount of Olives, and heard the fine answer that came from his father and the fine answer that he gave his father again.

Then she saw how our Lord went to his disciples and bade them wake up, for his enemies were near. And then there came a multitude of people with many lights and many armed men with staves, swords and pole-axes to seek out our Lord Jesus Christ. Responding as a meek lamb, our merciful Lord said to them, 'Whom do you seek?'

They answered in a rough mood, 'Jesus of Nazareth'.

Our Lord replied, '*Ego sum*' [I am he].

Then she saw the Jews falling down on the ground, not able to stand up for fear, but presently they got up again and searched as they had done before. And our Lord asked, 'Whom do you seek?'

And they said again, 'Jesus of Nazareth'.

Our Lord answered, 'I am he.'

And soon she saw Judas arrive and kiss our Lord, and the Jews laid hands upon him most violently. The she and our Lady endured much sorrow and great pain to see the Lamb of Innocence so contemptuously handled and dragged about by his own people to whom he had been especially sent. And very soon the said creature saw with her ghostly eye the Jews putting a cloth over our Lord's eyes, beating and battering him on the head and striking him across his sweet mouth, shouting most cruelly at him, 'Tell us now, who hit you?'

They did not spare to spit in his face in the most shameful way that they could. And then our Lady and she who was her unworthy handmaiden for the time wept and sighed most bitterly, for the Jews treated their blessed Lord so foully and venomously and they did not spare to pull on his blessed ears and tear out the hairs from his beard.

And soon afterwards she saw them pull off his clothes and render him completely naked and then drag him along before them as if he had been the worst evil-doer in the whole world. And he went on most meekly before them, naked as a newborn baby, to a pillar of stone and spoke no word against them but he let them do and say what they would. And there they bound him to the pillar as tightly as they could and beat him on his fair white body with rods, with whips and with scourges.

And then she thought our Lady wept amazingly bitterly; and therefore the said creature had to weep and cry when she saw such spiritual visions in her soul as clearly and as truly as if they had actually taken place before her bodily sight, and she thought that our Lady and she were always together in seeing our Lord's pains.

She had such spiritual visions every Palm Sunday and every Good Friday and in many other ways too over a period of many years. And for this reason she cried and wept most bitterly and suffered much contempt and reproof in many a country.

And then our Lord said to her soul, 'Daughter, I suffered these sorrows and other pains of various kinds and many more for your love, more than any man can tell on earth. Therefore, daughter, you have good reason to love me very well, for I have bought your love most dearly.'

The Conversion of Margery's Son [*Book,* pp. 221–5]

The said creature had a son, a tall young man, dwelling with a respected burgess in Lynn, trading merchandise and sailing over the sea, whom she desired to draw away from the dangers of this wretched and unstable world, if her power might reach to that. Nevertheless, she did as much as was in her to do, and whenever she might meet him at leisure she counseled him many times to leave the world and follow Christ – so much so that he fled her company and would not meet with her gladly.

So, one time it happened that the mother met with her son although it was against his will and his intention at that time. And as she had done before, so now she spoke to him again that he should flee from the dangers of this world and not set his devotion nor his business so much upon it as he did. He did not consent to this but answered her back sharply. Somewhat moved herself with sharpness of spirit, she said, 'Now, since you will not leave the world on my advice, I charge you at my blessing at least keep your body clean from women's company until you take a wife, according to the law of the Church. And, if you do not, I pray God chastise you and punish you for it.'

They parted from each other, and soon afterwards the same young man went on business overseas; and then, what through evil entice-ment of other people and the folly of his own behaviour, he fell into the sin of lechery. Soon afterwards his colour changed, his face grew full of weals and pustules as if it were a leper's.[17]

Then he came home again to Lynn to his master with whom he had previously been living. His master put him out of his service, not for any fault which he found with him, but perhaps supposing from his face that he were a leper. The young man told wherever he liked how his mother had cursed him, for which reason, so he supposed, God punished him so grievously. Some people, knowing of his complaint and having compassion for his distress, came to his mother saying she had done great evil, for through her prayer God had taken vengeance on her own child. Taking little notice of their words, she let it pass as if it didn't matter to her until he would come and pray for grace himself. So at last, when he saw no other remedy he came to his mother, telling her of his misconduct, promising to be

---

[17] The association between leprosy and lechery was a common misconception during the Middle Ages. It would appear, however, that Margery's son is suffering from some kind of sexually transmitted disease rather than leprosy.

obedient to God and to her and to amend his fault through the help of God, avoiding all misbehaviour from that time forward, according to his power. He asked his mother for her blessing, and especially he entreated her to pray for him that our Lord of his high mercy would forgive him for having trespassed and would take away that great sickness for which people fled from his company and his fellowship as if he were a leper. For he supposed that the Lord had sent him that punishment because of her prayers, and he therefore trusted to be delivered of them by her prayers, if she would pray for him out of charity. Then, having trust in his amending, and compassion for his infirmity, with sharp words of correction she promised to fulfil his purpose if God would grant it.

When she came to her meditation, not forgetting the fruit of her womb, she asked forgiveness for his sin and release from the sickness which our Lord had given him, if it were his pleasure and of profit to his soul. She prayed for so long that he was completely delivered from the sickness and lived for many years after and had a wife and a child – blessed must God be – for he married his wife in Prussia, in Germany.

*

A few years after this young man had married, he came home to England to his father and mother completely changed in his dress and disposition. Whereas in previous times his clothes were all dagged and his conversation all vanity,[18] now he wore no dagged clothes and his talk was full of virtue. Being greatly amazed at this sudden change, his mother said to him, 'Blessings, son, how is it that you are so changed?'

'Mother,' he said, 'I hope that our Lord has drawn me to him through your prayers, and I intend by the grace of God to follow your advice more than I have done before.' On seeing this wonderful influence of our Lord, his mother then thanked God as she could, paying close attention to his behaviour in case he was pretending. The longer that she observed his behaviour the more steadfast she thought he was and the more reverent towards our Lord. When she knew it was the pull of our Lord's mercy, then she was very joyful, thanking God many times for his grace and his goodness. After-

---

18   This is a reference to the popular fashion of the time whereby garments were cut along the edges to produce long, pointed projections. Earlier in the narrative, Margery has associated her own former adoption of dagged garments and gold-piped headdresses with the sin of pride and worldliness.

wards, in order for him to be more diligent and more busy to follow where our Lord would draw him she opened her heart to him, showing him and informing him how our Lord had drawn her to him through his mercy and by what means, also how much grace he had showed for her, all of which he said he was unworthy to hear. Then he went on many pilgrimages to Rome and to many other holy places to purchase pardon for himself, returning again to his wife and his child, as he was bound to do. He informed his wife about his mother, so much so that she wanted to leave her father and mother and her own country in order to come to England and see his mother. He was very glad of this and sent word to England to his mother to inform her of his wife's desire and to find out whether his mother would advise him to come by land or by water, for he trusted much in his mother's counsel, believing it was of the Holy Ghost. When his mother had a letter from him and knew his desire, she went to pray to find out our Lord's counsel and our Lord's will. And as she prayed for the said matter, it was answered in her soul that whether her son came by land or by water he should arrive safely. Then she wrote letters to him, saying that whether he came by land or water he should come in safety by the grace of God.

When he was informed of his mother's advice, he enquired when ships would come to England and hired a ship, or else part of a ship, in which he put his goods, his wife, his child and himself, proposing to come to England all together. When they were in the ship there arose such storms that they did not dare put to sea and so they came on land again, both he and his wife and their child. Then they left their child in Prussia with their friends, and he and his wife came to England overland to his father and his mother. When they arrived there, his mother greatly rejoiced in our Lord that her feeling was true, for she had a feeling in her soul, as is written before, that whether they came by land or by water they should come in safety. And so it was indeed, blessed must God be.

They came home on the Saturday in good health, and on the next day, that was the Sunday, while they were eating their meal at noon with other good friends, he fell very ill so that he rose from the table and lay down on a bed. This sickness and infirmity occupied him about a month and then in good life and right belief he passed to the mercy of our Lord. So, spiritually and bodily it might be well verified that 'he shall come home in safety' – which means not only into this mortal land, but also into the land of living men, where death shall never appear.

Curing the Woman with Post-Partum Sickness [*Book*, pp. 177–9]

As the said creature was in a Church of Saint Margaret to say her devotions, there came a man who knelt behind her, wringing his hands and showing signs of great distress. Perceiving his distress, she asked him what was troubling him. He said that things were very hard for him, for his wife had just had a child and was out of her mind. 'And madam,' he said, 'she doesn't know me or any of her neighbours. She roars and cries so that she terrifies people. She'll both hit out and bite, for which reason she is chained by the wrists.'

The she asked the man if he wanted her to go with him to see her, and he said, 'Yes madam, for God's love.' So she went with him to see the woman. And when she entered the house, as soon as the sick woman who was out of her mind saw her she spoke to her rationally and kindly and said she was very welcome to her. And she was very glad for her coming and greatly comforted by her presence, 'For you are', she said, 'a very good woman, and I see many fair angels around you, and therefore, I pray you, do not leave me, for I am greatly comforted by you.'

And, when other people came to her, she cried and gaped as if she would have devoured them and said that she saw many devils about them. She would not allow them to touch her willingly. She roared and cried so much for the most part of night and day that people would not endure her to live amongst them, she was so tedious to them. Then she was removed to a room in the farthest end of the town so that the people should not hear her crying. And there she was bound by hands and feet with chains of iron so that she could not hit anybody.

And the said creature visited her once or twice each day at least; and while she was with her she was meek enough and heard her talk and chat with good will without any roaring or crying. And the said creature prayed for this woman every day that God should, if it were his will, restore her to her senses again. And our Lord answered in her soul and said, 'She will live very well.' Then she was bolder in praying for her recovery than she was before, and each day, weeping and sorrowing, she prayed for her recovery until God returned her to her senses and her mind. And then she was brought to church and purified as are other women, blessed may God be.

In the opinion of those who knew of it, it was a very great miracle, for he who wrote this book had never before that time seen man or woman, as he thought, so removed from herself as was this woman, nor so difficult to control or to govern; and afterwards he saw her serious and sober enough – worship and praise be to our Lord without end for his high mercy and his goodness, who always helps at time of need.

II. Discourses of Desire

Desire for Celibate Marriage [*Book*, pp. 11–13]
This episode comprises Margery's first experience of mystical ecstasy. It appears to form the catalyst for a subsequent desire to live chastely, a constant need to talk about and contemplate spiritual matters, and for the expression of her gift of tears.

One night, as this creature lay in her bed with her husband, she heard a melodious sound so sweet and delectable she thought, as if she had been in paradise.[1] And immediately she jumped up our of her bed and said, 'Alas that ever I sinned; it is very merry in heaven.' This melody was so sweet that it surpassed all the melody that might be heard in this world without any comparison; and whenever she heard any mirth or melody afterwards it caused this creature to weep very plenteous and abundant tears of high devotion with great sobbings and sighings for the bliss of heaven, not fearing the shames and contempt of this wretched world. And forever after being drawn to God in this way, she was mindful of the mirth and the melody that was in heaven, so much so that she could not restrain herself very well from speaking of it. For when she was in any company, she would often say, 'It is very merry in heaven.'

Those who knew of her previous behaviour and now heard her speak so much about the bliss of heaven said to her, 'Why do you speak so about the mirth that is in heaven? You do not know it and you haven't been there any more than we have,' and they were very angry with her because she would not hear or speak of worldly things as they did, and as she had done before that time.

And after this time she never had any desire for sex with her husband, for the matrimonial debt was so abominable to her that she would have preferred, or so she thought, to eat or drink the slime, the muck in the gutter than to agree to any sexual contact, except only for obedience. And so she said to her husband, 'I may not deny you

---

The sound of angelic singing is one of the oldest recorded expressions of mystical ecstasy within the Christian tradition.

my body, but the love of my heart and my affection is drawn from all earthly creatures and set only on God.'

However, he would have his will, and she obeyed with great weeping and sorrowing because she might not live chastely. And this creature often urged her husband to live in chastity and said she knew well that they had frequently displeased God by their inordinate love and the great delight that each of them had in using the other's body, and now it would be good if they should by mutual will and consent punish and chastise themselves voluntarily by abstaining from the lust of their bodies. Her husband said that it would be good to do so, but he might not yet; he would when God willed it. And so he used her as he had done before, he would not desist. And all the time she prayed to God that she might live chastely, and three or four years afterwards, when it pleased our Lord, he made a vow of chastity, as shall be written about afterwards, by Jesus' leave.

And also, after this creature heard this heavenly melody, she performed great bodily penance. She was sometimes shriven twice or three times in one day and especially of that sin which she had concealed and covered up for so long, as is written in the beginning of the book. She gave herself to great fasting and to the keeping of long vigils; she rose at two or three o'clock and went to church and was there at her prayers until noon and also throughout the afternoon. And then she was slandered and disparaged by many people for her disciplined way of living. Then she obtained a hair cloth from a kiln – the type which people use to dry malt on – and wore it inside her bodice as discreetly and secretly as she could so that her husband should not see it; nor did he although she lay beside him every night in his bed and she wore the hair-shirt every day and bore children during that time.

Then she had three years of great difficulty with temptations which she bore as meekly as she could, thanking our Lord for all his gifts, and was as merry when she was reproved, scorned or ridiculed for our Lord's love, and much more merry than she had previously been when esteemed by the world. For she knew very well that she had sinned greatly against God and deserved more shame and sorrow than anybody could cause her, and that scorn for the worldly was the right way towards heaven, for Christ himself had chosen that way.

An Attempt at Adulterous Liaison [*Book*, pp. 13–16]

For the first two years when this creature was drawn to our Lord in this way, she had great quiet of spirit and was free from temptations. She could well endure fasting – it did not trouble her. She hated worldly joys. She felt no fleshly rebellion. She considered herself so strong that she feared no devil in hell, for she performed such great bodily penance. She thought that she loved God more than he did her. She was smitten with the deadly wound of vainglory and didn't feel it, for many times she desired that the crucifix should loosen his hands from the cross and hold her in token of love. Seeing this creature's presumption, our merciful Lord Christ Jesus sent her three years of great temptations, as is written before, one of the severest of which I intend to write about as an example to those who come after, so that they should not trust in their own selves nor have joy in themselves, as had this creature. For undoubtedly, our spiritual enemy does not sleep, but he very busily searches our temperament and inclinations, and wherever he finds us most frail, by our Lord's sufferance there he lays his snare, which nobody can escape by his own power.

And so he laid before this creature the snare of lechery when she believed that all fleshly lust had been completely quenched in her. And she was tempted so long with the sin of lechery in spite of anything that she could do about it. And yet she was often shriven, she wore the hair shirt and underwent great bodily penance and wept many a bitter tear and prayed very often to our Lord that he should preserve her and keep her so that she should not fall into temptation, for she thought she would rather be dead than to consent to it. And in all this time she had no physical desire for sex with her husband; on the contrary, it was very painful and horrible to her.

In the second year of her temptations it happened that a man whom she liked well said to her on St. Margaret's Eve[2] before evensong that he would give anything to sleep with her and enjoy his body's lust, and she should not resist him; for if he might not have his desire that time, he said, he would have it another time instead – she should not choose. And he did it to test what she would do, but she believed that he had meant it in full earnest at that time, and said little in reply. So they then parted and both went to hear evensong, for her church was that of Saint Margaret.

This woman was so preoccupied with the man's words that she could not listen to evensong nor say her *Our Father* nor think any

2   Saint Margaret of Antioch was a legendary virgin martyr, highly popular in late medieval England and one of the virgin saints much loved by Margery. She was also, appropriately, the patron saint of Margery's Church in Bishop's Lynn. The feast day of Saint Margaret was 20th July, and it is highly significant that Margery's temptation to adultery should coincide with this date.

other good thought, but was more troubled than ever she was before. The devil put it into her mind that God had forsaken her, or else she would not have been tempted in this way. She believed the devil's persuasions and began to consent because she was unable to think any good thought. She therefore believed that God had forsaken her, and when evensong was over she went to the aforesaid man so that he should have his lustful desire as she believed he wanted, but he dissimulated so much that she could not understand his intent, and so they separated for that night. This creature was so troubled and vexed all that night that she did not know what to do. She lay beside her husband and to have sex with him was so abominable to her that she could not bear it, and yet it was permissible for her and at a legitimate time if she had wanted to. But she was constantly preoccupied with sinning with the other man because he had spoken to her. At last, through the urgings of temptation and a lack of discretion, she was overcome and consented in her mind and went to the man to find out if he would then agree to have her. And he replied that he would not for all the money in the world; he would prefer to be chopped up as small as meat for the pot.

She went away thoroughly ashamed and confused in herself, seeing his steadfastness and her own instability. Then she was mindful of the grace that God had given her previously, how she had two years of great quiet in her soul, of repentance for her sin with many bitter tears of compunction and a perfect will never to turn again to her sin, but rather, she thought, to be dead. Then she fell half into despair. She thought she was in hell, such was the sorrow she had. She considered she deserved no mercy, for her consenting to sin was done so wilfully, nor was she worthy to serve God, for she had been so false to him.

Nevertheless, she was shriven many times and often and underwent whatever penance her confessor would enjoin her to do and was afterwards governed by the rules of the Church. That much grace God gave to this creature – blessed may he be – but he did not withdraw her temptation, but rather she thought that he increased it.

And she therefore believed that he had forsaken her, and she dared not trust to his mercy, but was vexed with horrible temptations of lechery and despair nearly all of the following year, except that our Lord in his mercy, as she said to herself, gave her each day for the most part two hours of compunction for her sins with many bitter tears. And afterwards she was tried with temptations of despair as she had been before and was as far from feelings of grace as those who had never felt any. And that she could not bear, and so she continued to despair. Except for the time when she felt grace, her trials were so amazing that she could only deal badly with them, but always mourned and sorrowed as though God had forsaken her.

A Vow of Marital Chastity [*Book*, pp. 23–5]

It happened on a Friday, on Midsummer's Eve in very hot weather,[3] that as this creature – who was carrying a bottle of beer in her hand – was travelling from York with her husband – who was carrying a cake inside his clothes – he asked his wife this question: 'Margery, if a man were to come here with a sword and wanted to cut off my head unless I should make love to you as I have done before, tell me truly in your conscience – for you say you will not lie – whether you would allow my head to be cut off or else allow me to make love to you again, as I did at one time?'

'Alas, Sir,' she said, 'why do you bring up this matter when we have been chaste for the past eight weeks?'

'Because I want to know the truth in your heart.'

And she said with great sorrow, 'Truly, I would rather see you killed than we should revert to our unclean behaviour.'

And he replied, 'You are no good wife.'

And then she asked her husband what was the cause of his not having had sex with her for the previous eight weeks, since she slept in his bed with him every night.

And he said he was made so fearful when he wanted to touch her that he dared not go further.

'Now, good sir, amend your ways and ask God mercy, for I told you nearly three years ago that you would suddenly be killed, and now this is the third year, and yet I hope I shall have my desire.[4] Good sir, I pray you to grant what I shall ask, and I shall pray for you that you shall be saved through the mercy of our Lord Jesus Christ, and you shall have more reward in heaven than if you wore a hair-shirt or a mail-coat. I pray you, allow me to make a vow of chastity in whatever bishop's hand that God wills.'

'No,' he said, 'I will not grant you that, for currently I may use your body without deadly sin, but then I would not be able to.'[5]

---

3 This is probably Midsummer's Eve 1413.
4 This refers to a time when Margery believed that God would strike her husband dead if he continued his sexual advances upon her.
5 Once a vow of chastity had been taken by a married couple and endorsed by the bishop, to renege on it was considered to be a deadly sin. On marital chastity see

Then she replied, 'If it be the will of the Holy Spirit to fulfil what I have said, I pray to God that you may consent to it; and if it is not the will of the Holy Spirit, I pray to God that you never consent to it.'

Then they travelled on towards Bridlington in very hot weather, the aforementioned creature having great sorrow and dread for her chastity. And as they came to a cross, her husband sat himself down under the cross, calling his wife to him and saying these words to her, 'Margery, grant me my desire and I will grant you your desire. My first desire is that we shall still sleep together in one bed as we have done before; the second is that you shall pay my debts before you go to Jerusalem; and the third is that you shall eat and drink with me on Fridays as you once used to do.'[6]

'No, sir,' she said, 'I will never grant you to break the Friday fast whilst I live.'

'Well,' he said, 'then I shall have sex with you again.'

She entreated him to give her leave to say her prayers and he kindly allowed it. Then she knelt down beside a cross in the field and prayed in this manner, with a great abundance of tears: 'Lord God, you know all things; you know what sorrow I have had to be chaste for you in my body for the past three years, and now I might have my will and I dare not, for love of you. For if I would break the way of fasting food and drink which you commanded me to undertake on Fridays, I should now have my desire. But, blessed Lord, you know I will not go against your will, and great is my sorrow now unless I find comfort in you. Now blessed Jesus, make your will known to my unworthy self so that I may follow it and fulfil it with all my strength.'

And then our Lord Jesus Christ spoke to this creature with great sweetness, commanding her to return to her husband and entreat him to grant her what she desired: 'And he shall have what he desires. For, my dearly beloved daughter, this was the reason for my bidding you

---

Dyan Elliott, *Spiritual Marriage: Sexual Abstinence in Medieval Wedlock* (Princeton, 1993). For a discussion of tensions within marriage caused by theological attitudes, see George Duby, *Love and Marriage in the Middle Ages* (Chicago, 1994), pp. 29–32.

6   Margery had already relinquished the eating of meat on Christ's instruction soon after her religious conversion and following a period of severe temptation. Her Friday fasts from food and drink, however, have been instigated by Christ some time before their York visit as a means of bargaining with John Kempe for a vow of chastity within their marriage.

to fast so that you should the sooner obtain and achieve your desire, and now it is granted to you. I no longer want you to fast; therefore I bid you in the name of Jesus to eat and drink as your husband does.'

Then this creature thanked our Lord Jesus Christ for his grace and goodness, and afterwards she rose up and went to her husband, saying to him, 'Sir, if it pleases you, you shall grant me my desire and you shall have your desire. Grant me that you shall not come into my bed and I grant you that I will pay off all your debts before I go to Jerusalem. And, make my body free to God, so that you never make any claims on me to fulfil the matrimonial debt after this day for as long as you live, and I shall eat and drink on Fridays at your bidding.'

Then her husband replied to her, 'May your body be as free to God as it has been to me.'

This creature thanked God greatly, rejoicing that she had her desire, praying her husband that they should say three *Our Fathers* in worship of the Trinity for the great grace that he had granted them. And so they did, kneeling under a cross, and afterwards they ate and drank together in great gladness of spirit. This was on a Friday on Midsummer's Eve.

Harassed by Fellow Pilgrims [*Book*, pp. 61–2]
Following her vow of chastity with her husband, made probably in June 1413, Margery sets off alone on pilgrimage to the Holy Land in the autumn of the same year.

This creature had eaten no meat and drunk no wine for four years before leaving England, and now, since her confessor directed her by virtue of obedience that she should both eat meat and drink wine, she did so for a little while. Afterwards, she entreated her confessor to excuse her if she ate no meat, and to allow her to do as she wished for what time he pleased.

And soon afterwards because of the stirrings of some of her company, her confessor was displeased because she ate no meat, and so was much of the company. And they were most displeased that she wept so much and always talked of the love and goodness of our Lord as much at the table as elsewhere. As a consequence, they shamefully reproved her, rebuking her thoroughly and said that they would not put up with her as her husband did when she was at home in England.

And she replied to them meekly, 'Our Lord, Almighty God is as great a lord here as in England, and I have just as much cause to love him here as I do there – blessed may he be.'

At these words her companions were angrier than they were

before and their fury and unkindness towards this creature was a matter of great unhappiness, for they were considered to be very good men and she greatly desired their love, if she might have had it to the pleasure of God. And then she said to one of them in particular, 'You cause me much shame and hurt.'

Presently he replied, 'I pray God that the devil's death may overtake you soon and quickly', and uttered many more cruel words to her than she could repeat. And soon afterwards some of the company whom she trusted best, as well as her own maid, also said that she could no longer travel in their company, and they threatened to take her maid from her so that she should not be branded a strumpet in her company. And one of them who had her gold in his safekeeping left her a noble with great anger and vexation to go where she would and care for herself as well as she might, for they said that she should no longer stay with them, and they abandoned her that night.

Then, on the next morning, one of the company came to her, a man who loved her well, praying that she would go to his companions and behave meekly towards them and entreat them to let her still remain in their company until she arrived at Constance. And so she did, and travelled on with them in great discomfort and trouble until she arrived at Constance, for they inflicted much shame and reproof upon her in various places as they went along. They cut her gown so short that it reached only a little below her knee, and made her put on some white canvas, like a sacking apron, so that she should be taken for a fool, and the people would not make much of her or hold her in any regard. They made her sit below all the others at the end of the table so that she hardly dared say a word.

And in spite of their malice, she was held in more esteem than they wherever they went. And although she sat at the lowest end of the table, the good man of the house where they lodged would always console her as much as he could in front of them all and sent her some of his own food, such as he had, and that very much annoyed her companions.

As they travelled towards Constance, they were told that they would be harmed and have great discomfort unless they had great grace. Then this creature came to a church and went in to pray, and she prayed with all her heart, with great weeping and many tears for help and succour against her enemies.

Presently, our Lord said to her mind, 'Do not be afraid, daughter; your companions will suffer no harm whilst you are in their company. And so they travelled on to Constance in safety – blessed may our Lord be in all his works.

Attempted Rape at Leicester [*Book*, pp. 112–13]

Whilst on a later pilgrimage to the north of England in 1417 Margery is arrested and threatened on a number of occasions, often impugned for her singular white clothing and as a woman travelling alone.

Then the Steward of Leicester, a good-looking man, sent to the jailer's wife for the said creature, and because her husband was not at home she would not release her to any man, steward or other. When the jailer knew of this he came to her personally and brought her before the steward. Then, as soon as he saw her, the steward spoke Latin to her, there being many priests and other people also standing about to hear what she had to say. She said to the steward, 'Speak English, if you please, for I cannot understand what you are saying.'

The steward said to her, 'You lie falsely, in plain English.'

Then she replied to him, 'Sir, ask whatever question you will in English and through the grace of my Lord Jesus Christ I shall answer you reasonably.'

And then he asked many questions, to which she responded readily and reasonably, so that he could not find any cause against her.

Then the steward took her by the hand and led her into his chamber and spoke many foul and ribald words to her, purposing and desiring, so it seemed to her, to overcome her and rape her. And then she experienced much fear and sorrow, begging him for mercy. She said, 'Sir, for the reverence of Almighty God, spare me, for I am a man's wife.'

And then the steward said, 'You shall tell me whether you have these words from God or from the devil, or else you shall go to prison.'

'Sir,' she said, 'I am not afraid to go to prison for my Lord's love, who suffered much more for my love than I may for his. I pray you, do as you think best.'

Seeing her boldness and that she was not afraid of imprisonment, the steward wrestled with her, making filthy gestures and indecent looks, by which he frightened her so much that she told him how she had her holy speech and her communication from the Holy Spirit and not from her own knowledge.

Entirely astonished by her words, he left off his intentions and his lewdness, saying to her as many men had done before, 'Either you are truly a good woman or else a very wicked one', and he delivered her back to her jailer who took her home with him again.

Threatened Rape at Aachen [*Book*, pp. 235–7]

Margery's pilgrimage to Aachen – one undertaken without the permission of her confessor – takes place during a trip she embarks upon to accompany her recently bereaved daughter-in-law home to Germany. By this stage Margery is in her sixties, is partially disabled, and is here travelling with whatever company she can find.

They did not stay long in the said place, but in a short time they made their way towards Aachen, riding in carts until they came to a river where there was a great gathering of people, some heading towards Aachen and some to other places. Among them was a monk, a very reckless and undisciplined man, and in his company were some young men who were merchants. The monk and the merchants knew the man who was this creature's guide well, and called him by his name, and showed very good humour towards him.

When they had crossed the water and went back onto the land, the monk and the merchants, the said creature with her guide, all in a company together in a cart, came past a house of Friars Minor,[7] and they were all suffering great thirst. They bade the said creature go in to the friars and get them some wine. She said, 'Sirs, you will excuse me, for if it were a house of nuns I would go very readily, but in as much as they are men, I shall not go, by your leave.'

So one of the merchants went and fetched a bottle of wine for them. Then some friars came to them and entreated them to come and view the blessed sacrament in their church, for it was within the Octave of Corpus Christi,[8] and it stood open in a crystal vessel so that people might gaze on it if they wanted to.

The monk and the men went with the friars to view the precious sacrament. The said creature thought she would see it as well as them and followed after, although it was against their will. And when she saw the precious sacrament, our Lord gave her so much sweetness and devotion that she wept and sobbed amazingly bitterly and was not able to restrain herself from doing so. The monk and all her

---

7   This is an unidentified house of Franciscans situated somewhere between Wilsnack (from where Margery is travelling), and Aachen.
8   Corpus Christi is a moveable feast which is celebrated on the Thursday after Trinity Sunday. Margery was probably in Aachen during the eight days of this festival in 1433 or 1434. During the course of the festival the sacrament was frequently put on display in a glass casket, as seems to have been the case here. For an extended examination of the Corpus Christi festival and its associations in the Middle Ages see Miri Rubin, *Corpus Christi: The Eucharist in Late Medieval Culture* (Cambridge, 1991).

company were angry because she wept so bitterly and when they returned to their cart they chastised and rebuked her, calling her a hypocrite and said other many evil words to her. In order to excuse herself she quoted scripture against them, verses from the Psalter '*Qui seminant in lacrimis*' etc., '*euntes ibant & flebant*' etc. [They who sow in tears etc. They who go forth and cry etc.][9] and other such phrases. Then they were even angrier and said that she should no longer travel on in their company and persuaded her guide to forsake her. Gently and meekly she entreated them to allow her to travel on in their company for God's love and not to leave her alone where she knew nobody and nobody knew her wherever she should go.

With great prayer and pleading she travelled on with them until they came to a fine town during the Octave of Corpus Christi. And there they said that on no account whatsoever should she go with them any longer. He who was her guide, who had promised to take her back to England, abandoned her, delivering back her gold and such things as he had in his safekeeping, and promising to lend her more gold if she had wanted. She said to him, 'John, I did not want your gold; I would prefer to have had your company in these strange lands rather than all your money, and I believe you would please God more to go with me as you promised me at Danzig than if you went to Rome on foot.'

Thus they cast her out of their company and let her go where she would. Then she said to him who had been her guide, 'John, you forsake me for no other reason but that I weep when I see the sacrament and when I think of our Lord's Passion. And, since I am forsaken for God's cause, I believe that God shall provide for me and deliver me as he would himself, for he has never deceived me – blessed must he be.'

So they went on their way and left her there still. The night fell upon her and she was very wretched, for she was alone. She did not know with whom she might rest that night, nor with whom she might journey the next day.

Some priests of that country approached her where she lodged. They called her Englishwoman with a tail,[10] and spoke many lewd words to her, with filthy gestures and looks, proposing to lead her

---

9   Psalm 126: 5–6.
10   The Middle English term is 'sterte' – a word with sexual connotation and refer-
     ring to an old insult on the continent which identified the English as possessors
     of tails.

about if she wanted. She had much fear for her chastity and was very unhappy.

Then she approached the good wife of the house, entreating her to let some of her maids sleep with her that night. The good wife assigned two maids who remained with her all night, yet she dared not sleep for fear of being defiled. She stayed awake and prayed nearly all that night that she might be preserved from all uncleanness and meet up with some good company which might help her on to Aachen. Suddenly, she was commanded in her soul to go to church early the next day and there she would meet with some company.

Early the next day she paid for her lodging, inquiring of her hosts if they knew of any company travelling towards Aachen. They said, 'No'. Taking her leave of them, she went to church to discover and prove if her feeling were true or not.

When she arrived there, she saw a company of poor people. Then she went up to one of them, inquiring where they purposed to go. He said, 'To Aachen'. She entreated him to allow her to travel in his company.

'Why, lady,' he said, 'have you no man to accompany you?'

'No,' she said, 'my man has left me.'

So she was received into a company of poor people, and when they arrived in any town she bought her own food and her companions went about begging. When they were outside the towns, her companions took off their clothes and, sitting naked, picked them for vermin. Need compelled her to wait for them and prolong her journey and to be put to much more expense that she would otherwise have been. This creature was too embarrassed to remove her clothes as did her fellows and as a result, through her association with them, caught some of their vermin and was dreadfully bitten and stung both day and night until God sent her other companions. She remained in their company with great anguish and discomfort and much delay until the time came when they arrived in Aachen.

Sexual Temptation [*Book*, pp. 144–5]

Just as we saw in Margery's earlier attempt at adulterous liaison, she is frequently tormented by sexual temptation. On this occasion, temptation is brought about by her failure to trust in God's counsel.

Thus, through hearing holy books read and through listening to holy sermons she was always increasing her contemplation and holy meditation. It would be impossible to write all the holy thoughts, holy speeches and the high revelations which our Lord showed her, both concerning herself and other men and women, and also concerning many souls, some of whom would be saved and some of whom would be damned. This was a great punishment and sharp chastisement to her. For she was very glad and joyful to know of those who would be saved, for she desired as much as she dared for all people to be saved, and when our Lord revealed to her any that would be damned, she felt great pain. She would not listen to it nor believe that it was God who revealed such things to her, and she put it out of her mind as much as she might. Our Lord blamed her for this and bade her believe that it was his high mercy and his goodness to show her his secret counsels, saying to her mind, 'Daughter, you must hear of the damned as well as of the saved.'

However, she would give no credence to God's counsel, but instead she believed it was some evil spirit intent on deceiving her. Then for her presumptuousness and her disbelief, our Lord drew from her all good thoughts and all mindfulness of holy speeches, communications and the high contemplation which she had been used to before, and imposed upon her as many evil thoughts as previously she had had good thoughts. And this torment lasted for twelve days altogether, and just as in previous times she had spent four hours before noon engaged in holy speeches and communications with our Lord, so had she now as many hours of foul thoughts and foul recollections of lechery and all filth, as if she should have become a common prostitute to all types of people.

And so the devil took her in hand, toying with her with cursed thoughts, just as our Lord had communed with her previously with holy thoughts. And just as she had had previously many glorious visions and high contemplations upon the manhood of our Lord, upon our Lady and upon many other holy saints, so now – for anything she could do about it – she had horrible and abominable visions in which she saw men's naked genitals and other such abominations. She thought she saw many different men of religion, priests and many others both heathen and Christian coming before her sight and showing her their naked genitals, so that she could not avoid them nor put them out of her sight. And at this the devil urged her in her mind to choose which one of them all she would have first, for she must be had in common by them all. And he said she liked some of them better than all the others and she thought he spoke the truth; she could not refuse and had to do his bidding – and yet she would not have done it for all this world. But yet she thought that it should be done, and against her will she thought that these horrible sights and cursed recollections were delightful to her. Wherever she went or whatever she did, these cursed thoughts stayed with her. When she would see the sacrament, make her prayers or do any other good deed, such cursed thoughts were always put in her mind. She was shriven and did all she could, but she found no release until she was nearly in despair. The pain she was in and the sorrow that she felt cannot be written.

Identification with Mary Magdalene [*Book*, p. 197]

From the time of her Jerusalem pilgrimage onwards, Margery identifies strongly with Mary Magdalene who thereafter often figures in her visions and contemplations.

[I]n her contemplation, the creature was with Mary Magdalene, sorrowing and seeking our Lord at the grave, and she heard and saw how our Lord Jesus Christ appeared to her in the likeness of a gardener, saying, 'Woman, why are you weeping?'

Not knowing who he was and all inflamed with the fire of love, Mary said to him again, 'Sir, if you have taken away my Lord, tell me, and I shall take him back again.'

Then our merciful Lord, having pity and compassion on her, said, 'Mary'.

And, knowing it was our Lord, with that word she fell down at his feet and would have kissed his feet, saying, 'Master'.

Our Lord said to her, 'Touch me not.'

Then the creature thought that Mary Magdalene said to our Lord, 'Ah, Lord, I see clearly that you will not have me be as intimate with you as I have been before', and looked very downcast.

'Yes, Mary,' said our Lord, 'I shall never forsake you, but I shall always be with you, without end.'

And then our Lord said to Mary Magdalene, 'Go tell my brethren and Peter that I have risen.'

And then the creature thought that Mary went forth with great joy, and that it was a great marvel to her that Mary rejoiced, for if our Lord had spoken to her as he did to Mary, she thought she could never have been happy. That was when she would have kissed his feet and he said, 'Touch me not.' The creature had such great grief and sorrow at those words that whenever she heard them in a sermon as she did many times, she wept, sorrowed and cried as if she should have died, for the love and desire that she had to be with our Lord.

Professions of Love: Spiritual Virginity [*Book*, pp. 50–3]

As this creature lay in contemplation, weeping sorrowfully in her spirit, she said to our Lord Jesus Christ, 'Ah, Lord, there are virgins now dancing happily in heaven. Shall I not do so? For because I am not a virgin, lack of virginity is now a great sorrow to me; I think I would rather have been put to death when I was taken from the font than I should ever have displeased you. And then you, blessed Lord, would have had my virginity without end. Ah, dear God, I have not loved you all the days of my life, and that sorely grieves me. I have run away from you and you have run after me. I would fall into despair but you would not let me.'

'Ah, daughter, how often have I told you that your sins are forgiven you and that we are joined together without end? You are especially loved, daughter, and therefore I promise you that you shall have an individual grace in heaven, daughter; and I promise you that I shall come to your end, at your dying, with my blessed mother and my holy angels and twelve apostles, Saint Katherine, Saint Margaret, Saint Mary Magdalene and many other saints who are in heaven, who give me great worship for the grace which I as your God, your Lord Jesus, give to you. You do not need to fear any grievous pains at your dying, for you shall have your desire, which is to be more aware of my Passion than of your own pain. You shall not dread the devil of hell, for he has no power over you. He fears you more than you do him. He is angry with you, for you torment him more with your weeping than do all the fires in hell. You win many souls from him with your weeping. And I have promised you that you shall endure no other purgatory than the slanderous talk of the world, for I have chastised you myself as I wished to, with many great fears and torments of evil spirits, which you have endured both sleeping and waking for many years. For this reason I shall preserve you at your end through my mercy, so that they shall have no power over you, neither in body nor in soul. It is a great sign of grace and a miracle that you still have your bodily wits, in view of the vexation that you have suffered from them in the past.

'I have also chastised you, daughter, with the fear of my Godhead, and many times I have frightened you with great tempests and winds, so that you thought that vengeance should fall on you because of your sin. I have tested you by means of many tribulations, many great griefs, and many grievous sicknesses, so much so that you have been anointed for death, and you have escaped entirely through my grace. Therefore do not be afraid, daughter, for with my own hands which were nailed to the cross I shall take your soul from your body with great joy and melody, with sweet smells and pleasant odours, and offer it to my father in heaven, where you shall see him face to face, dwelling with him without end.

'Daughter, you shall be most welcome to my father and to my mother and to all my saints in heaven, for you have given them drink many times with tears of your eyes. All my holy saints will rejoice in your coming home. You shall be fulfilled with all kinds of love which you desire. Then you will bless the time when you were made and the body that has dearly purchased you. He shall rejoice in you and you in him without end.

'Daughter, I promise you the same grace that I promised Saint Katherine, Saint Margaret, Saint Barbara[11] and Saint Paul, so that if any creature on earth until the Day of Judgement asks any boon of you and believes that God loves you, he shall have his boon, or else something better. Therefore, those who believe that God loves you shall be endlessly blessed. The souls in purgatory will rejoice in your coming home, for they know well that God loves you especially. And on earth, people will rejoice in God for you, for he shall work much grace for you and make all the world know that God loves you. You have been despised for my love and therefore you shall be worshipped for my love.

'Daughter, when you are in heaven, you may ask what you will and I shall grant you all your desire. I have told you before that you are a special lover of God and for that reason you shall have a special love in heaven, a singular reward and a singular worship. And, because you are a virgin in your soul, I shall take you by the one hand in heaven and my mother by the other hand, and so shall you dance in heaven with other holy maidens and virgins, for I may call you dearly bought and my own beloved darling. I shall say to you, my own blessed spouse, "Welcome to me with all manner of joy and gladness to dwell here with me and never to depart from me without end, but ever to dwell with me in joy and bliss, which no eye may see, no ear may hear, no tongue may tell, no heart may think, what I have ordained for you and for all my servants who desire to love me and please me as you do."'

---

11 Like Saint Margaret, Saint Katherine and Saint Barbara were legendary virgin martyrs also highly popular in the Middle Ages. Saints Margaret and Katherine appear on a number of other occasions in Margery's narrative, Saint Barbara on this one occasion only. Saint Barbara was the patron saint of sudden death.

Professions of Love: *Sponsa Christi* [*Book*, pp. 213–14]

'You have suffered much shame and much reproof and therefore you shall have very much bliss in heaven. Daughter, do not be ashamed to receive my grace when I will give it to you, for I shall not be ashamed of you, so that you shall be received into the bliss of heaven. There, for every good thought, for every good word, and for every good deed, and for every day of contemplation, and for all the good desires which you have had here in this world, you will be rewarded with me everlastingly as my dearly beloved darling, as my blessed spouse and as my holy wife.

'And therefore do not be afraid, daughter, although the people wonder why you weep so bitterly when you receive me, for, if they knew what grace I put in you at that time they would rather wonder why your heart did not break apart. And so it should if I did not measure that grace myself; but you see well yourself, daughter, that when you have received me into your soul you are in peace and quiet and sob no longer. And for this the people have great wonder, but it need be of no surprise to you, for you know well that I behave like a husband who would marry a wife. At the time when he marries her he thinks he is sure enough of her and that nobody shall set them apart, for then, daughter, they may go to bed together without any shame or fear of people's opinion and sleep in rest and peace if they will. And things are like this between you and me, daughter, for every week, especially on a Sunday, you have great fear and dread in your soul how you may best be sure of my love; and with great reverence and holy dread you fear how you may best receive me to the salvation of your soul with all kinds of meekness, humility and charity, as any lady in this world is busy to receive her husband when he comes home and has been away from her for a long time.

'My dearly beloved daughter, I thank you highly for all those people whom you have kept safe in my name, and for all the goodness and service that you have done them in any degree, for you shall have the same reward with me in heaven as if you had cared for my own self whilst I was here on earth. Also, daughter, I thank you for as many times as you have bathed me in your soul at home in your chamber as though I had been present in my manhood, for I know well, daughter, all the holy thoughts that you have shown me in your mind. And also, daughter, I thank you for all the times that you have harboured me and my blessed mother in your bed. For these and all other good thoughts and good deeds that you have thought in my name and performed for my love, you shall have with me and with my mother, with my holy angels, with my apostles, with my martyrs, confessors and virgins and with all my holy saints, all manner of everlasting joy and bliss.'

Marriage to the Godhead (*Book*, pp. 86–92)

As this creature was in the church of the Holy Apostles in Rome on Saint Lateran's Day,[12] the Father of Heaven said to her, 'Daughter, I am well pleased with you inasmuch as you believe in all the sacraments of the Holy Church and in all faith involved with that, and especially because you believe in the manhood of my son and for the great compassion which you have for his bitter Passion.'

The Father also said to this creature, 'Daughter, I will have you wedded to my Godhead, for I shall show you my secrets and my counsels, for you shall live with me without end.'

Then the creature remained silent in her soul and gave no answer to this, for she was very much afraid of the Godhead and she had no comprehension of the communing of the Godhead, for all her love and all her affection were fixed on the manhood of Christ and of that she had good knowledge and she would not have parted from that for anything.

She loved the manhood of Christ so much that when she saw women in Rome carrying children in their arms, if she found out that any were boys, she would then cry, roar and weep as though she had seen Christ in his childhood. And if she could have had her will, often she would have taken the children out of their mothers' arms and have kissed them instead of Christ. And if she saw a handsome man, it gave her great pain to look at him lest she might see him who was both God and man. And she therefore cried many times and often when she met a handsome man and wept and sobbed very bitterly for the manhood of Christ as she went about in the streets of Rome, so that those who saw her were very much amazed by her for they did not know the cause.

Therefore, it was not surprising that she remained still and did not answer the Father of Heaven when he told her that she should be wedded to his Godhead. Then the Second Person, Jesus Christ, whose manhood she loved so much, said to her, 'Margery, my daughter, what do you say to my father in response to these words which he speaks to you? Are you well pleased that it should be so?'

12 This church (originally dedicated to saints Philip and James), visited by Margery whilst on pilgrimage, was replaced in the eighteenth century. This episode took place on Saint John Lateran's day, 9th November 1414.

Then she would not answer the Second Person but wept amazingly bitterly, desiring to have him still and in no way to be parted from him. Then the Second Person in the Trinity answered his father for her, saying, 'Father, excuse her, for she is still young and not fully conversant with how she should answer.'

And then the Father took her by the hand in her soul before the Son and the Holy Ghost and the Mother of Jesus and all the twelve apostles and Saint Katherine and Saint Margaret and many other saints and holy virgins with a great multitude of angels, saying to her soul, 'I take you, Margery, for my wedded wife, for fairer, for fouler, for richer, for poorer, provided you be obedient and meek in doing what I command you to do. For, daughter, there was never a child so kind to its mother as I shall be to you, both in joy and in sorrow, to help you and comfort you. And that I pledge to you.'

And then the Mother of God and all the saints who were present in her soul prayed that they might have much joy together. And then the creature thanked God for this spiritual comfort with high devotion and with a great many tears, considering herself in her own estimation highly unworthy of any such grace as she felt, for she felt many great comforts, both spiritual comforts and bodily comforts. Sometimes she sensed sweet smells with her nose; she thought they were sweeter than any sweet thing on earth that she ever smelled before, nor might she ever tell how sweet they were, for she thought she might have lived on them, had they lasted.

Sometimes she heard with her bodily ears such sounds and melodies that she could not hear what a man said to her at that time unless he spoke louder. These sounds and melodies she had heard nearly every day for as long as fifteen years when this book was written, and particularly when she was in devout prayer, also many times whilst she was both in Rome and England.

With her bodily eyes she saw many white things flying all about her on every side, as thick in a way as dust in the sunlight; they were very delicate and comforting and the brighter the sun shone, the better she could see them. She saw them at many different times and in many different places, both in church and in her chamber, at her meals and at her prayers, in the country and in the town, both moving about and whilst sitting down. And she was frequently afraid what they might be, for she saw them as clearly in the darkness of the night as she did in daylight. Then, when she was afraid of them, our Lord said to her, 'By this token, daughter, believe it is God who speaks to you, for wherever God is, heaven is, and wherever God is, there are many angels, and God is in you, and you are in him. And therefore do not be afraid, daughter, for these signify that you have many angels about you to protect you both day and night, so that no devil shall have power over you, nor evil man to harm you.' Then from that time forward, when she saw them coming she used to say, '*Benedictus qui venit in nomine domini*' [Blessed is he who comes in the name of the Lord]. Our Lord also gave her another token which lasted about sixteen years, and it increased continually, more and more; and that was a flame of fire, amazingly hot and delectable and very comforting, never waning but the flame ever increasing. For although the weather were never so cold, she felt the heat burning in her breast and at her heart, as truly as a person would feel the material fire if he put his hand or his finger into it.

When she first felt the fire of love burning in her breast she was afraid of it, and then our Lord answered in her mind, and said, 'Daughter, do not be afraid, for this heat is the heat of the Holy Ghost which shall burn away all your sins, for the fire of love quenches all sins. And you shall understand by this token that the Holy Ghost is within you, and you know well that wherever the Holy Ghost is, there is the Father, and where the Father is, there is the Son, and so you have all the Holy Trinity fully in your soul. Therefore you have great cause to love me very well, and yet you shall have a greater reason to love me than ever you have had, for you shall hear things you never heard, and you shall see things you never saw, and you shall feel things you never felt. For, daughter, you are as sure of the love of God as God is God. Your soul is more sure of the love of God than of your own body, for your soul shall separate from your body but God shall never part from your soul, for they are united together without end.

'Therefore, daughter, you have as great a reason to be happy as any lady in this world; and if you knew, daughter, how much you please me when you willingly allow me to speak in you, you should never do otherwise, for this is a holy life and the time is very well spent. For, daughter, this life pleases me more than the wearing of a coat of mail,[13] or a hair-shirt, or fasting on bread and water; for even if you were to say a thousand *Our Fathers* every day you should not please me as well as you do when you are silent and allow me to speak to you in your soul.

---

13 The Middle English used here is 'habergeon', referring to the coat of chain-mail which was often worn as a garment of penance. See also the redacted text, p. 127 for its inclusion of this passage.

*

'Fasting, daughter, is good for young beginners, and discreet penance, especially what their confessor gives them or enjoins them to do. And to say many beads is good for those who can do no better,[14] and yet it is not perfect. But it is a good route towards perfection. For I tell you, daughter, those who are great fasters and great penitents want that to be considered the best life; also, those who give themselves to saying many devotions want that to be considered the best way of life; and those who donate many alms, they want that to be held as the best way of life.

'And I have often told you, daughter, that thinking, weeping and high contemplation is the best life on earth. And you shall have more merit in heaven for one year of thinking in your mind than for a hundred years of praying with your mouth, and yet you will not believe me, for you will pray many beads, whether I want you to or not. And yet, daughter, I will not be displeased with you whether you think, say or speak, for I am always pleased with you.

'And if I were on earth as bodily as I was before I died on the cross, I should not be ashamed of you as many other people are, for I would take you by the hand amongst the people and greet you warmly so that they would know well that I loved you very much.

'For it is appropriate for the wife to be intimate with her husband. However great a lord he might be, and she so poor a woman when he marries her, yet they must lie together and rest together in joy and peace. Just so must it be between you and me, for I take no notice of what you have been, but what you would be. And I have often told you that I have clean forgiven all your sins. Therefore, I must be intimate with you and lie in your bed with you. Daughter, you greatly desire to see me and when you are in bed you may boldly take me to you as your wedded husband, as your beloved darling and as your sweet son, for I want to be loved as a son should be loved by his mother and want you to love me, daughter, as a good wife ought to love her husband. And therefore you may boldly take me in the arms of your soul and kiss my mouth, my head and my feet as sweetly as you want. And as often as you think about me or would do any good deed to me, you shall have the same reward in heaven as if you did it to my own precious body which is in heaven, for I ask no more of you but for your heart to love me who loves you, for my love is always ready for you.'

[14] Here Christ is referring to the saying of the rosary.

Then she gave thanks and praise to our Lord Jesus Christ for the high grace and mercy that he showed to her, an unworthy wretch.

This creature had a variety of tokens in her bodily hearing. One was a kind of sound like a pair of bellows blowing in her ear. Being afraid of this, she was warned in her soul not to be afraid, for it was the sound of the Holy Ghost. And then our Lord turned that sound into the voice of a dove and afterwards he turned it into the voice of a little bird which is called a redbreast which often sang very merrily in her right ear. And then she would always have great grace after hearing such a token. And she had been used to such tokens for about twenty-five years at the time of writing this book.

Then, our Lord Jesus Christ said to his creature, 'By these tokens you may well know that I love you, for you are a true mother to me and to all the world because of that great charity that is in you, and yet I am myself the cause of that charity, and you shall therefore have great reward in heaven.'

III. Voice and Authority

Prophesy on Demand [*Book*, pp. 55–8]

In order to verify this creature's feelings, the priest who wrote this book asked her questions many different times about things that were to come, things of which the outcome was unsure and of which nobody was certain at that time. Although she was reluctant and unwilling to do such things, he entreated her to pray to God about them and, when our Lord would visit her with devotion, to find out what the outcome would be, and to tell him truly without any pretence how she felt, or else he would not gladly have written the book.

And so, partly compelled by fear that he would otherwise not have followed her intention to write this book, this creature did as he entreated her and told him her feelings about what should happen in such matters as he asked her about, to discover whether her feelings were true. And in this way he tested them for their truth. And yet he would not always give credence to her words, and that hindered him in the following way.

It happened once that a young man whom this priest had never seen before came to him complaining about the poverty and disease into which he had fallen by bad luck, explaining the cause of the mischance, saying too that he had taken holy orders to be a priest. Out of a little hastiness to defend himself – he claimed he had no choice or else he would have been pursued and killed by his enemies – he struck a man, or else two, as a result of which, as he said, they were dead or else likely to die. And so he had fallen into violation of his holy orders and might not execute his orders without dispensation from the court of Rome, and for this reason he fled from his friends and dared not enter his own part of the country for fear of being arrested for their deaths.

The said priest gave credence to the young man's words because he was a likeable person, handsome, well-favoured in appearance and manner, sober in his language and talk, priestly in his gesture and clothing. Having compassion for his trouble and intending to get him some friends to relieve and comfort him, he went to a respectable citizen in Lynn, the equal of a mayor and a merciful man, who lay very sick and had done so for a long time. He complained to him and to his wife, a very good woman, about the bad luck of this young man, trusting that he would receive generous alms, as he had often done for others for whom he had asked.

It happened that the creature about whom this book is written was present there and heard how the priest complained of the young man's problem and how he praised him. And she was deeply moved in her spirit against that young man, and said that they had many poor neighbours whom they knew well enough had need of being helped and relieved, and that more alms were needed to help those whom they knew well to be well-disposed folk and their own neighbours, rather than other strangers whom they did not know, for many people speak and appear outwardly fair to people's sight – but God knows what they are in their souls.

The good man and his wife thought she spoke very well and as a result they would give him no alms. At that time the priest was very displeased with this creature and when he met with her alone, he repeated how she had prevented him from getting alms for the young man who, in his opinion, was a well-disposed man, and he much commended his behaviour.

The creature said, 'Sir, God knows what his behaviour is, for as far as I know I never saw him. And yet I have an understanding of what his behaviour might be, and therefore, sir, if you will follow my counsel according to what I feel, let him decide and help himself as well as he can and don't you get involved with him, for he will deceive you in the end.'

The young man was always returning to the priest, flattering him and saying that he had good friends in other places who would help him if they knew where he was, and in a short time too, and they would also thank those people who had supported him in his trouble. Trusting it would be as this young man told him, the priest willingly lent him silver to help him out. The young man asked the priest to excuse him if he did not see him for two or three days, for he was going a little way away and would return shortly and bring back his silver, truly. Having confidence in his promise, the priest was very content, granting him good love and leave until the day when he had promised to return.

When he had gone, the said creature had an understanding by feeling in her soul that our Lord would reveal that he was a dishonest man and that he would not come back any more. In order to prove whether her feeling was true or false, she asked the priest where the young man was whom he had praised so much. The priest said that he had gone a little way away and he trusted that he would return again. She said she supposed that he would see no more of him, nor did he ever see him again. And then he was sorry that he had not followed her advice.

A short time after this happened, another dishonest villain, an old man, came to the same priest and offered to sell him a breviary, a good little book. The priest went to the said creature, entreating her to pray for him to find out whether God wanted him to buy the book or not. And while she prayed, he encouraged the man as well as he could and afterwards he returned to this creature and asked her how she felt.

'Sir,' she said, 'do not buy a book from him, for he is not to be trusted and you will know that well if you get involved with him.'

Then the priest asked the man if he could see the book. The man replied that he did not have it on him. The priest asked how he came by it. He answered that he was executor to a priest who had been related to him and he had charged him to sell it and dispose of it for him.

'Father,' said the priest out of reverence, 'why do you offer me this book rather than other men or other priests when there are many thriftier, richer priests in this church than I am and I know well that you never had any previous knowledge of me.'

'Truly, sir,' he said, 'I certainly didn't. Nevertheless, I feel good will towards you, and also it was the will of its previous owner that if I knew any young priest whom I considered sober and well-disposed, that he should be offered this book before anyone else for a lower price than any other person, so that he might pray for him. And these reasons made me come to you rather than to another man.'

The priest asked where he lived.

'Sir,' he said, 'only five miles from this place at Pentney Abbey.'[1]

'I have been there', said the priest, 'and I have not seen you.'

'No, sir,' he replied, 'I have only been there only a short time and now I have a provision of food there – God be thanked.'

The priest asked him if he could see the book and if they might come to an agreement.

He said, 'Sir, I hope to be here again next week and to bring it with

---

[1] Situated about seven miles to the south-east of Lynn, Pentney Abbey was an Augustinian priory dedicated to the Holy Trinity, the Virgin Mary and Mary Magdalene.

me. And, sir, I promise that you shall have it before anyone else, if you like it.'

The priest thanked him for his benevolence, and so they parted, but the man never returned to the priest afterwards, and then the priest knew well that the said creature's feeling was true.

Saving the Church of Saint Margaret from fire [*Book*, pp. 162–4]

Once, there happened to be a great fire in Bishop's Lynn which burnt down the Guildhall of the Trinity. And in the same town this hideous and grievous fire threatened to burn the parish church dedicated in honour to Saint Margaret, a solemn and richly honoured place, and also the whole town, had there been no grace or miracle.[2]

The said creature, being present there and seeing the dangerous plight of the whole town, cried very loudly many times that day and wept very copiously, praying for grace and mercy for all the people. And notwithstanding that at other times they could not endure her crying and weeping for the plentiful grace that our Lord wrought in her, on this day in order to avoid their physical danger they suffered her to cry and weep as much as she wanted to, and nobody would order her to stop; rather they entreated her to continue, fully trusting and believing that through her crying and weeping our Lord would take them to mercy.

Then her confessor came to her and asked if it were best to carry the sacrament towards the fire or not. She replied, 'Yes, sir, yes! For our Lord Jesus Christ told me it will be well.'

So her confessor, the parish priest of St Margaret's Church, took the precious sacrament and went before the fire as devoutly as he could and afterwards brought it again to the church, and the sparks of the fire flew about the church. The said creature, desiring to follow the precious sacrament to the fire, went out of the church door, and, as soon as she saw the hideous flames of fire, immediately she cried with a loud voice and great weeping, 'Good Lord, make things well.'

These words worked in her mind, inasmuch as our Lord had said to her before that he would make things well, and therefore she cried, 'Good Lord, make things well and send down some rain or some

---

[2] According to the report of this fire as documented in H. Harrod, *Report on the Deeds and Records of the Borough of King's Lynn* (King's Lynn, 1874), p. 28, the conflagration occurred on the night of 23 January, 1421. Cited in Meech and Allen, *Book*, p. 327, n. 162/29–31.

weather which may, by your mercy, quench this fire and ease my heart.'

Afterwards, she went back into the church, and then she saw how the sparks came into the choir through the lantern of the church. Then she had a new sorrow and cried very loudly again for grace and mercy with a great many tears. Soon afterwards, three worthy men came in to her with white snow on their clothes, saying to her, 'See, Margery, God has shown us great grace and sent us a fair fall of snow with which to quench the fire. Be happy now and thank God for it.'

And with a great cry she offered praise and thanks to God for his great mercy and his goodness, and especially because he had said to her before that all should be very well when it was very unlikely to be well, except by a miracle and special grace. And now that she saw that it was well indeed, she thought that she had great cause to thank our Lord.

Then her confessor[3] came to her and said he believed that God granted them to be delivered out of their great dangers because of her prayers, for without devout prayers it could not happen that the air, being bright and clear, should be changed so soon into clouds and darkness and send down great flakes of snow by which the fire was hindered in its natural working – blessed must our Lord be.

Trial and Self-Defence at York [*Book*, pp. 123–8]
This pilgrimage of Margery's to York is undertaken following her eventful and highly threatening visit to Leicester.[4]

There was a monk who was going to preach in York who had heard much slander and much evil talk about the said creature. And when he was going to preach, there was a great crowd of people to hear him and she was present there with them. And so, when he embarked upon his sermon, he recounted many matters so openly that the people saw perfectly well that it was on account of her, for which those friends who loved her well were very sorry and upset about it. But she was much the happier because she had something to try her patience and her charity, through which she trusted she might please our Lord Jesus Christ.

---

3   This is probably Robert Spryngolde, Margery's principal confessor and parish priest of Saint Margaret's Church in Bishop's Lynn. His faith in Margery's powers to deliver them from danger here is unusual since he tends to be far more cautiously disposed towards her claims.

4   See p. 62 above.

When the sermon was over, a doctor of divinity who loved her well, came to her – as did many other people too – and said, 'Margery, how have you been doing today?'

'Sir,' she said, 'very well indeed, blessed be God. I have cause to be very happy and glad in my soul that I may suffer anything for his love, for he suffered much more for me.'

Afterwards there came a good-willed man who loved her very well. Along with his wife and others he led her seven miles from there to the Archbishop of York[5] and brought her into a fine chamber where a clerk came and said to the good man who had brought her there, 'Sir, why have you and your wife brought this woman here? She will steal away from you and then you will incur shame because of her.'

The good man said, 'I dare well say she will remain and answer for herself most willingly.'

On the next day she was brought into the Archbishop's chapel and there came many of the Archbishop's household, scorning her, calling her 'Lollard' and 'heretic', and swearing many a horrible oath that she should be burned. And through the strength of Jesus she replied to them, 'Sirs, I fear you shall be burned in hell without end unless you correct yourselves of your swearing, for you do not keep God's commandments. I would not swear as you do for all the money in the world.'

Then they went away as if they were ashamed. Then, saying her prayers in her mind, she asked for grace to be humiliated that day as was most pleasure to God and of profit to her own soul, and it would provide a good example to her fellow Christians. In answer, Our Lord said that all would be very well.

At last, the Archbishop came into the chapel with his clerks and said to her sharply, 'Why do you go about in white? Are you a virgin?'

Kneeling before him, she said, 'No, sir, I am no virgin; I am a wife.'

He commanded his household to fetch a pair of fetters and said she would be fettered because she was a false heretic. And then she said, 'I am no heretic, nor shall you prove me one.'

The Archbishop went away and let her stand alone. Then she

---

5 The Archbishop at York at this time was Henry Bowet who was renowned for his zeal against Lollardy. His seat at Cawood, to where Margery is taken, is approximately nine miles south of the Minster.

prayed for a long while to our Lord God Almighty to help her and sustain her against all her enemies, both spiritual and physical, and her flesh trembled and quaked amazingly, so that she was glad to put her hands under her garments so that it should not be noticed.

Afterwards, the Archbishop returned to the chapel with many worthy clerks, amongst whom was the same doctor who had examined her before and the monk who had preached against her a little time before at York. Some of the people asked whether she were a Christian woman or a Jew; some said she was a good woman and some said she was not.

Then the Archbishop took his seat, as did his clerks, each according to his status, many people being present. And whilst the people were gathering together and the Archbishop was taking his seat, the said creature stood at the back, praying with high devotion for help and succour against her enemies for so long that she melted all into tears. And in the end she cried out loudly, so that the Archbishop and his clerks and many people were greatly amazed at her, for they had not heard such crying before.

When her crying passed, she came before the Archbishop and fell down on her knees, the Archbishop saying very roughly to her, 'Why do you weep so, woman?'

In reply she said, 'Sir, you shall wish one day that you had wept as bitterly as I.'

And then at once, after the Archbishop put to her the Articles of our Faith – to which God gave her grace to answer well and truly and readily without any great thought, so that he could not criticise her. Then he said to the clerks, 'She knows her faith well enough. What shall I do with her?'

The clerks said, 'We know very well that she knows the Articles of the Faith, but we will not allow her to live amongst us because the people have great faith in her communications and perhaps she might lead some of them astray.

Then the Archbishop said to her, 'I have been told very bad things about you. I hear it said that you are a very wicked woman.'

And she replied, 'Sir, in the same way I also hear it said that you are a wicked man. And if you are as wicked as people say, you shall never come to heaven, unless you amend your ways whilst you are here.'

Then he said aggressively, 'Why, you! What do people say about me?'

She answered, 'Other people can tell you well enough.'

Then a great clerk with a furred hood said, 'Be quiet! You speak about yourself and let him be!'

Afterwards, the Archbishop said to her, 'Lay your hand on the book before me here and swear that you will leave my diocese as soon as you can.'

'No, sir,' she said, 'I pray you to permit me to go back into York to take leave of my friends.'

Then he gave her permission for a day or two. She thought it was too short a time, so she replied, 'Sir, I may not leave the diocese so hastily, for I must stay and speak with good people before I go. And, sir, with your permission, I must go to Bridlington and speak with my confessor, a good man, who was the confessor to the good Prior, who is now canonised.'[6]

Then the Archbishop said to her, 'You shall swear that you will not teach or challenge the people in my diocese.'

'No, sir, I shall not swear,' she said, 'for I shall speak of God and rebuke those who swear great oaths wherever I go until the time that the Pope and Holy Church have ordained that nobody shall be so bold as to speak of God, for God Almighty does not forbid, sir, that we speak of him. And also the Gospel makes mention that when the woman had heard our Lord preach, she came before him with a loud voice and said,

"Blessed be the womb which bore you and the breasts that gave you suck." Then our Lord said again to her, "Truly they are blessed who hear the word of God and keep it."[7] And therefore, sir, I think that the Gospel gives me leave to speak of God.'

'Ah, sir,' said the clerks, 'We know well that she has a devil within her, for she speaks of the Gospel.'[8]

A great clerk quickly brought forward a book and quoted Saint Paul for his part against her that no woman should preach.[9]

In answer to this, she said, 'I do not preach, sir, nor do I enter any

---

6   Here Margery is referring to William Sleighholme who was confessor to John Slaytham, later Saint John of Bridlington, who had been canonised in 1401. It is likely that Margery was intent on travelling to his shrine in order to make her confession there.

7   Luke 11: 27–8.

8   The implication is that Margery has been engaging in Lollard studies of the Bible in the vernacular, something still outlawed unless on licence.

9   Presumably this passage is one taken from I Corinthians 14: 34–5, a passage frequently invoked in order to silence troublesome women.

pulpit. I use only communication and good words, and that will I do as long as I live.'

Then a doctor who had examined her previously said, 'Sir, she told me the worst tale about priests that I ever heard.'

The Archbishop commanded her to tell that tale.

'Sir, by your reverence, I only spoke of one priest by way of example, who as I have learned of it, went astray in a wood through God's sufferance, for the profit of his soul, until night came upon him. Lacking any shelter, he found a beautiful arbour in which he rested that night, which had a lovely pear-tree in the middle laden and adorned with blossom and flowers most delightful to his sight. A great vicious bear, ugly to behold, came there and shook the pear-tree, causing the flowers to fall down. This horrible beast greedily ate and devoured those fair flowers. And when he had eaten them, he turned his tail towards the pricst and defecated them out again at his rear end.

'The priest was greatly revolted by that disgusting sight, becoming very depressed for uncertainty of what it might mean. On the next day he wandered off on his way all heavy and pensive, and happened to meet a good-looking old man like a pilgrim who asked the priest the reason for his sadness. Recounting the matter written about before, the priest said he experienced great fear and sadness when he saw that loathsome beast soil and devour such beautiful flowers and blossoms, and afterwards discharge them from his tail-end so horribly in front of him, and he did not understand what this might mean.

Then the pilgrim, showing himself to be the messenger of God, addressed him in this way: 'Priest, you yourself are the pear-tree flourishing and flowering through your saying of services and administering the sacraments, although you do so without devotion, for you take very little heed how you say Matins and other services, as long as it is babbled to an end. Then you go to your mass without devotion and you have very little contrition for your sin. There you receive the fruit of everlasting life, the sacrament of the altar, with a very feeble attitude. All day long afterwards you misspend your time, you give yourself to buying and selling, bargaining and exchanging as if you were a man of the world. You sit over your beer, giving your-self up to gluttony and excess, to the lust of your body through lechery and impurity. You break God's commandments through swearing, lying, detraction, backbiting and other such sins. Thus, through your misconduct, just like the loathsome bear, you devour and destroy the flowers and blooms of virtuous living, to your endless damnation and to the hindrance of many other people, unless you have grace for repentance and the amendment of your ways.'

Then the Archbishop liked the tale very much and commended it, saying it was a good tale. And the clerk who had examined her previously in the Archbishop's absence said, 'Sir, this tale cuts me to the heart.'

The said creature said to the clerk, 'Ah, worthy doctor, sir, in the place where I live most of the time there is a worthy clerk, a good preacher who boldly speaks against the misbehaviour of the people, and who will flatter nobody. He says many times in the pulpit, "If anybody is displeased by my preaching, note him well, for he is guilty." And just so, sir,' she said to the clerk, 'do you behave with me – God forgive you for it.'

The clerk did not know well what to say to her. Afterwards, the same clerk came to her and begged her forgiveness for having been so against her. Also, he entreated her especially to pray for him.

And then afterwards the Archbishop said, 'Where shall I get a man to lead this woman away from me?'

Quickly there jumped up many young men and every one of them said, 'My lord, I will go with her.'

The Archbishop answered, 'You are too young; I will not have you do it.'

Then a good, sober man from the Archbishop's household asked his lord what he would give him if he would escort her. The Archbishop offered him five shillings and the man asked for a noble. In reply, the Archbishop said, 'I will not spend so much on her body.'

'Yes, good sir,' said this creature, 'Our Lord shall reward you very well again.'

Then the Archbishop said to the man, 'See, here is five shillings. Lead her quickly out of this area.'

Kneeling down, she asked him his blessing. Entreating her to pray for him, he blessed her and let her go. Then, going again to York, she was received by many people and by very worthy clerks who rejoiced in our Lord, who had given her – uneducated as she was – the wit and wisdom to answer so many learned men without shame or blame – thanks be to God.

Preaching and Trial at Beverley [*Book*, pp. 129–31]
Upon leaving York, Margery journeys on to Hull where she receives much abuse. She is rescued by a good man who takes her into his protection for a little while. However, because of the malicious demands of the people, he is forced to send her away again.

On the next morning her host led her out to the edge of the town, for he dared not keep her with him any longer. And so she went to Hessle and would have crossed over the river Humber. Then she happened to find there two Preaching Friars and two yeomen of the Duke of Bedford.[10] The friars told the yeomen which woman she was and the yeomen arrested her as she was about to board her boat, and they also arrested a man who was travelling with her.

'For our lord, the Duke of Bedford, has sent for you', they said. 'And you are considered the greatest Lollard in all this land, and around London too. And we have been searching for you in many parts of the land and we shall have a hundred pounds for bringing you before our lord.'

She said to them, 'Sirs, I shall willingly go with you where you will lead me.'

Then they brought her back to Hessle, and there the people called her Lollard and women came running out of their houses with their distaffs crying to the people, 'Burn this false heretic.'

So, as she went on towards Beverley with the said yeomen and the aforementioned friars, they met many times with the people of that area who said to her, 'Woman, give up this life which you lead and go spin and card wool as other women do, and do not suffer so much shame and unhappiness. We would not suffer so much for anything on earth.'

Then she said to them, 'I do not suffer as much sorrow as I would do for our Lord's love, for I suffer only sharp words, and our merciful Lord Jesus Christ – worshipped be his name – suffered hard lashes, bitter scourgings and shameful death at the end for me and for all mankind – blessed may he be. And therefore it is truly nothing that I suffer in comparison to what he suffered.'

And so, as she went along with the said men she told them good tales until one of the Duke's men who had arrested her said to her, 'I regret that I met with you, for it seems to me that you speak very good words.'

Then she said to him, 'Sir, do not regret or repent that you met with me. Do your lord's will and I trust that all will turn out for the best, for I am very pleased that you met with me.'

---

10 The Duke of Bedford was the third son of Henry IV and at this time would have been Lieutenant of the Kingdom during Henry V's protracted absence whilst in France. He was also an anti-Lollard campaigner and was present at the execution of John Oldcastle, the so-called 'father of Lollardy'. Significantly, his two yeomen will accuse Margery of being Oldcastle's daughter: see p. 88 below.

He replied, 'Woman, if ever you become a saint in heaven, pray for me.'

She answered, saying to him, 'Sir, I hope you shall be a saint yourself, and everybody who shall enter heaven.'

So they went on until they arrived in Beverley where the wife of one of the men who arrested her lived. And they led her there and took away her purse and her ring from her. They arranged for her a pleasant room with a decent bed in it, with all the necessary things, locking the door with the key and taking the key away with them.

Afterwards they took the man whom they arrested with her, who was the Archbishop of York's man, and put him in prison. And soon after that, on the same day there came news that the Archbishop was coming to the town where his man had been put in prison. The Archbishop was informed of his man's imprisonment and immediately he had him let out.

Then that man went to the said creature with an angry demeanour, saying, 'Alas, that ever I knew you! I have been imprisoned because of you.'

Comforting him, she replied, 'Be meek and patient and you shall have great reward in heaven because of it.'

So he went away from her. Then she stood looking out at a window and told many good tales to those who would hear her, so much so that women wept bitterly and said with great heaviness of their hearts, 'Alas, woman, why should you be burned?'

Then she entreated the good wife of the house to give her a drink, for she was desperately thirsty. And the good wife said that her husband had taken away the key, for which reason she was unable to come to her and give her a drink. And then the women took a ladder and set it up against the window and gave her a pint of wine in a pot and took her a cup, entreating her to hide the pot and the cup so that when the good man returned he might not notice it.

*

On the next day she was brought into the Chapterhouse of Beverley and there was the Archbishop of York and many great clerks with him – priests, canons and secular men. Then the Archbishop said to this creature, 'What, woman, have you come before me again? I would rather be rid of you.'

And then a priest brought her before him and the Archbishop said in the hearing of everybody present, 'Sirs, I had this woman before me at Cawood where I examined her in her faith with my clerks and found no fault in her. Furthermore, sirs, since that time I have spoken with good men who consider her a perfect woman and a good woman. Notwithstanding all this, I gave one of my men five shillings to escort her out of this area in order to quieten down the people. And as they were on their journey, they were taken and arrested. My man was put in prison because of her, and her gold and silver was also taken away from her along with her beads and her ring, and now she is brought here before me again. Is there anybody here who can speak against her?'

Then, other men said, 'Here is a friar who knows many things against her.'

The friar came forward and said that she disparaged all men of Holy Church[11] and he uttered much evil language against her at that time. He also said that she would have been burnt at Lynn had his order, that is the Preaching Friars, not have been there.[12] 'And, sir, she says that she may weep and have contrition when she will.'

Then two men who had arrested her came, saying along with the friar that she was Cobham's daughter and was sent to carry letters about the country.[13] And they said she had not been to Jerusalem nor the Holy Land nor on any other pilgrimage as she had been in reality. They denied all truth and maintained what was wrong, as many others had done before. When they had said enough for a long while, they held their peace.

Then the Archbishop said to her, 'Woman, what is your answer to all this?'

She said, 'My lord, saving your reverence, all the words that they say are lies.'

Then the Archbishop said to the friar, 'Friar, the words are not heresy; they are slanderous words and erroneous.'

'My lord,' said the friar, 'she knows her faith well enough. Nevertheless, my Lord of Bedford is angry with her and he will get her.'

'Well, friar,' said the Archbishop, 'and you shall escort her to him.'

'No, sir,' said the friar, 'it is not a friar's duty to lead a woman about.'

'And', said the Archbishop, 'I do not want the Duke of Bedford to be angry with me on her account.'

---

11 Anti-clericalism was one of the most notorious of Lollard tendencies.
12 The reference here is to the Dominican order of monks established in Bishop's Lynn in the reign of Henry III.
13 John Oldcastle was also known as Lord Cobham. The implication here is that Margery is one of Oldcastle's missionaries.

Then the Archbishop said to his men, 'Watch the friar until I want to examine him again', and he commanded another man to guard the said creature also until he would examine her again another time when he pleased. The said creature entreated his lordship that she should not be put amongst men, for she was a man's wife. And the Archbishop said, 'No, you shall not come to any harm.'

Then he who was charged with her took her by the hand and led her home to his house and made her sit with him to eat and drink, making her most welcome. Soon afterwards there came many priests and other people to see her and speak with her, and many people had great compassion that she was treated so badly.

A short time later, the Archbishop sent for her and she came into his residence. His household was dining and she was led into his chamber, even up to his bedside. Then, bowing, she thanked him for his gracious favour that he had shown to her previously.

'Yes, yes,' said the Archbishop, 'I hear worse things about you than ever before.'

She said, 'My lord, if you please to examine me, I shall admit the truth, and if I be found guilty I will obey your correction.'

Then a Preaching Friar who was a Suffragan[14] with the Archbishop came forward to whom the Archbishop said, 'Now, sir, just as you said to me when she was not present, say now whilst she is present.'

'Shall I do so?' said the Suffragan.

'Yes', said the Archbishop.

'Then the Suffragan said to this creature, 'You were at my Lady Westmorland's, Miss.'[15]

'When, Sir?' she said.

'At Easter', said the Suffragan.

Not answering this, she said, 'Well, sir?'

Then he said, 'My Lady herself was very pleased with you and

---

[14] An assistant or subsidiary bishop performing episcopal functions, but with little or no jurisdiction. He was able to be summoned upon by the Archbishop to attend ecclesiastical courts, or else to offer his suffrage when necessary.

[15] Lady Westmorland was Joan Beaufort, daughter of John of Gaunt. John of Gaunt was sympathetic to the Lollard cause, suggesting that Margery may have had stronger Lollard connections than has been appreciated. This connection is further corroborated by the fact that whilst in London after her Prussian pilgrimage in old age, she is entertained with people who have come from the house of the Cardinal Priest of Saint Eusebius. This Cardinal was none other than Henry Beaufort, legitimated son of John of Gaunt and brother of Lady Westmorland. For the account of this visit, see pp. 99–101 below.

liked your words well, but you advised my Lady Greystoke[16] to leave her husband, and she is a baron's wife and daughter to Lady Westmorland, and now you have said enough to be burned for.' And so he multiplied many sharp words in front of the Archbishop – it is not fitting to repeat them.

At last she said to the Archbishop, 'My lord, if it is your will, I have not seen my Lady Westmorland these two years and more. Sir, she sent for me before I went to Jerusalem, and if it pleases you I will go again to her to corroborate that I incited no such thing.'

'No,' said those who stood about, 'let her be put in prison and we shall send a letter to the worthy lady, and, if she speaks the truth, let her go free without any danger.' And she said she was very satisfied that it should be so.

Then a great clerk who stood a little to one side of the Archbishop said, 'Put her in prison for forty days and she will love God the better whilst she lives.'

The Archbishop asked her what tale it was that she had told the Lady of Westmorland when she spoke with her.

She said, 'I told her a good tale of a lady who was damned because she would not love her enemies, and of a bailiff who was saved because he loved his enemies and forgave them their trespasses against him, and yet he was held to be an evil man.'

The Archbishop said it was a good tale. Then his steward and many more people with him cried in a loud voice to the Archbishop, 'Lord, we beg you to let her go from here this time, and if ever she comes back again, we shall burn her ourselves.'

The Archbishop said, 'I believe there was never a woman in England so treated as she is and has been.' Then he said to this creature, 'I do not know what I shall do with you.'

She said, 'My lord, I pray you, let me have your letter and your seal as a record that I have exonerated myself against my enemies and nothing is charged against me, neither error nor heresy that may be proved, thanks be our Lord. And again allow John, your man, to lead me over the river.'

And the Archbishop granted all her desire most kindly – may God grant him his reward – and delivered to her her purse with her ring and beads which the Duke of Bedford's men had taken from her before. The Archbishop was amazed at where she got the means to

16 Lady Greystoke was daughter to Joan Beaufort (and hence granddaughter to John of Gaunt), and was married to John de Greystoke in 1407.

travel about the country and she said that good people gave it to her so that she would pray for them.

Kneeling down, she then received his blessing and gladly took her leave as she left his chamber. And the Archbishop's household entreated her to pray for them, but the steward was angry because she laughed and was cheerful, saying to her, 'Holy people should not laugh.'

She said, 'Sir, I have great reason to laugh, for the more shame and scorn I suffer, the happier I may be in our Lord Jesus Christ.'

Then she came down into the hall and there stood the Preaching Friar who had caused her all that trouble. And so she passed by with one of the Archbishop's men, carrying the letter which the Archbishop had granted her for a testimony. He escorted her to the Humber estuary, where he took his leave of her, returning to his lord and carrying the said letter with him again, so that she was left alone without any knowledge of the people.

All of this trouble happened to her on a Friday – thanks be to God for everything.

Seeking Oral Authority [*Book*, pp. 41–3]
In the face of perpetual scepticism and disbelief on the part of many of her contemporaries, Margery continually seeks out authority in order to validate her mystical powers and revelations.

This creature was charged and commanded in her soul to go to a White Friar called William Southfield in the same city of Norwich,[17] a good man who lived a holy life, to show to him the grace that God had wrought in her, just as she had done to the good vicar previously.[18] She did as she was commanded, and arrived at the friar's one morning, and spent a long time with him in the chapel, and revealed to him her meditations and what God had wrought in her soul, to ascertain if she had been deceived by any illusions or not.

Holding up his hands all the time whilst she told of her feelings, this good man, this White Friar, said, 'Jesus, mercy and goodness! Sister, do not be afraid of your way of living, for it is the Holy Ghost

---

[17] William Southfield was a Carmelite friar of Norwich who was subject to mystical experiences – specifically visitations from the Virgin Mary.

[18] This refers to a visit made by Margery to Richard Caister, vicar of St Stephen's Church in Norwich. At first showing cynicism about Margery's abilities, Caister eventually became her confessor during her visits to Norwich. Caister died in 1420 and his tomb reputedly became the site of miracles.

working his grace abundantly in your soul. Thank him highly for his goodness, for we are all bound to thank him for you, who now in our times inspires his grace in you well, so that you may be of help and comfort to us all who are supported by your prayers and by others like you. And we are preserved from many misfortunes and troubles which we should deservedly suffer for our misdeeds, if there were not such good creatures in our midst. Blessed be Almighty God for his goodness. And therefore, sister, I advise you to dispose yourself to receive God's gifts as humbly and meekly as you can, and offer up no obstacle or objection to the goodness of the Holy Ghost, for he may distribute his gifts where he wants to, and makes worthy the unworthy, and righteous the sinful. His mercy is always readily available for us unless we are ourselves guilty, for he does not inhabit a body which is subject to sin. He flies from all feigning and falsehood; he asks of us a humble, meek and contrite heart with a good will. Our Lord himself says, "My Spirit shall alight upon a meek man, a contrite man and one who fears my words." Sister, I trust in our Lord that you have these conditions in your will, your affection, or in both, and I do not consider that our Lord will allow those to be endlessly deceived who put all their trust in him and neither seek nor desire anything other than him, as I hope is the case with you. And therefore you may fully believe that our Lord loves you and is working his grace in you. I pray God increase it and continue it to his everlasting worship and for his mercy.'

The aforementioned creature was greatly comforted both physically and spiritually by the words of this good man and was considerably strengthened in her faith.

And then she was commanded by our Lord to visit an anchoress by the name of Dame Julian[19] living in the same city. And so she did, and revealed to her the grace that God had put in her soul, of the compunction, contrition, sweetness and devotion, compassion with holy meditation and high contemplation, and all the many holy words and dalliances which our Lord spoke to her soul; and she revealed many of her wonderful revelations to the anchoress to determine if there was any deceit in them, for the anchoress was expert in such matters and was able to offer good advice.

---

[19] Julian of Norwich (1343–c. 1414) received a series of visions during a life-threatening illness in 1373 which she seems to have spent much of her life documenting in two texts. She appears to have entered the anchorhold attached to St Julian's Church in Norwich at some stage during the 1390s and Margery's visit to her would suggest that she had attracted at least a local following.

On hearing the marvellous goodness of our Lord, the anchoress thanked God highly with all her heart for his visitation, advising this creature to be obedient to our Lord God's will and to fulfil with all her might whatever he put in her soul as long as it was not contrary to God's worship and to the profit of her fellow Christians; for if it were, then it would not be the influence of a good spirit but rather would belong to an evil spirit.

'The Holy Ghost never urges anything which is opposed to charity, and if he did he would be opposing his own self, for he is all charity. Also, he moves a soul to complete chastity, for those who live chastely are called the temple of the Holy Ghost, and the Holy Ghost makes a soul stable and steadfast in the correct faith and right belief. And a duplicitous man in his soul is always unstable and unsteadfast in all his ways. He who is forever in doubt is like the sea-flood which is shifted and borne about by the wind, and such a man is not likely to receive the gifts of God. Whatever creature does receive these tokens must steadfastly believe that the Holy Ghost dwells in his soul. And much more, when God visits a creature with tears of contrition, devotion or compassion, he may and ought to believe that the Holy Ghost is in his soul.

'Saint Paul says that the Holy Ghost asks for us with mourning and unspeakable weeping,[20] that is to say he makes us ask and pray with mourning and weeping so plentiful that the tears may not be numbered. No evil spirit may offer these tokens, for Jerome states that tears torment the devil more than do the pains of Hell.[21] God and the devil are eternally in opposition and they shall never live together in the same place, and the devil has no power in a man's soul. Holy Writ asserts that the soul of a righteous man is the seat of God, and so I trust, sister, that you are too. I pray God grant you perseverance. Put all your trust in God and do not fear the words of the world, for the more contempt, shame and reproof which you suffer in the world, the more is your merit in the sight of God. You must be patient, for in that way, you will preserve your soul.'

Much was the spiritual communion enjoyed by the anchoress and

---

20 Romans 8: 26.

21 No exact passage from the writings of St Jerome corresponds to this statement, but it may be that Julian is citing or paraphrasing a passage from *Speculum Christiani*, in which St Bernard is recorded as stating, 'Teres of a synnere turmente3 more the deuyl than alle kynde of turmentryes' [A sinner's tears torment the devil more than all kind of torments], EETS o.s. 182, ed. G. Holmstedt (London, 1933), p. 214 (my translation).

this creature through conversing about the love of our Lord Jesus Christ during the many days they spent together.

Seeking Scripted Authority [*Book*, pp. 142–4]

On one occasion, as this creature was in her contemplation, she hungered very much for God's word and said, 'Alas, Lord, with all the clerks you have in this world, you will not send me one of them to fill my soul with your word and with the reading of Holy Scripture, for all the clerks who preach may not fulfil me, for I think that my soul is always just as hungry. If I had enough money I would give a noble to have a sermon every day, for your word is worth more to me than all the money in this world. And therefore, blessed Lord, have pity on me, for you have taken away from me the anchorite who was a unique solace and comfort to me and who many times refreshed me with your holy word.'[22]

Then our Lord Jesus Christ answered in her soul, saying, 'There shall come one from far away who will fulfil your desire.'

So, many days after this answer, there came a priest who was new to Lynn and who had never known her before, and when he saw her going about in the streets he was greatly moved to speak with her and inquired of other people what type of woman she was. They said they trusted to God that she was a very good woman.

Afterwards, the priest sent for her, entreating her to come and speak with him and with his mother, for he had hired a room for his mother and for himself, and so they lived together. Then the said creature came to find out what he wanted, and spoke with his mother and with him and was very well received by them both.

Then the priest took up a book and read in it how our Lord wept on seeing the city of Jerusalem, recounting the misfortunes and sorrows that should befall it, 'for she knew not the time of her visitation'.[23] When the said creature heard it read how our Lord wept, then she wept bitterly and cried loudly, the priest and his mother not knowing any reason for her weeping. When her crying and weeping ceased, they rejoiced and were very happy in our Lord. Afterwards, she took her leave and parted from them at that time.

When she was gone, the priest said to his mother, 'I am much amazed at this woman – why she weeps and cries so. Nevertheless, I

---

22   This man, one of Margery's confessors who had obviously been of major support to Margery throughout her life, has evidently died. This is explicitly corroborated later in the *Book*. See Meech and Allen, *Book*, p. 168.

23   Luke 19: 41–4.

think she is a good woman and I very much desire to speak with her more.' His mother was very pleased and advised him to do so.

And afterwards the same priest loved and trusted her very much and blessed the time that ever he knew her, for he found great spiritual comfort in her and she caused him to look up much good scripture and many a good commentator, which he would not have done at that time had it not been for her.

He read to her many a good book of high contemplation and other books such as the Bible glossed by commentators, Saint Bridget's book, Hilton's book, Bonaventure's *Stimulus Amoris, Incendium Amoris* and others similar.[24] And then she knew that when she complained about the lack of reading, it was a spirit sent from God which said to her these words as written a little earlier, 'There shall come one from afar who shall fulfil your desire.' And thus she knew by experience that it was a very true spirit.

Female Solidarity [*Book*, pp. 93–5]
Whilst returning from Jerusalem, Margery finds herself abandoned and destitute in Rome. On this occasion, as on many others, salvation comes in the form of help and support from other women.

One night she saw in a vision how our Lady, or so she thought, sat at table with many worthy people and begged for food for her. And then this creature thought that our Lord's words were fulfilled spiritually in that vision, for a little before that time he had promised this creature that he would pray to his mother to beg on her behalf.

And a short time after this vision she met with a worthy lady, Dame Margaret Florentyne, the same lady who had brought her from Assisi to Rome.[25] Neither of them could understand the other very well, except by signs, gestures and a few words in common. And then this lady said to her, 'Margerya in poverté?'

Understanding what the lady meant, she replied 'Yea, grand poverté, Madame.'[26]

---

24 These books refer to the *Revelationes* of Saint Bridget, Walter Hilton's *Scale of Perfection*, the *Stimulus Amoris* (thought at the time to have been written by Saint Bonaventure but which in fact has been reattributed to one of the saint's Franciscan followers), and, of course, Rolle's *Incendium Amoris*.

25 This noblewoman had previously met with Margery at Assisi, following which encounter she had agreed to Margery joining her retinue for the return journey to Rome.

26 It would seem here that Margery is trying to render the question and its response into Italian.

Then the lady bade her eat with her every Sunday and placed her at her own table above herself, and served her her food with her own hands. Then this creature sat and wept very bitterly, thanking our Lord that she was so encouraged and cherished for his love by those who could not understand her language.

When they had eaten, the good lady used to take for her a hamper full of other stuff with which to make her own stew, enough to serve her with food for two days, and she filled her bottle with good wine. And sometimes she gave her eight Bolognan coins as well.[27]

And then another man in Rome, who was called Marcelle, invited her for meals two days a week. His wife was heavily pregnant and greatly desired this creature to be godmother to her child when it was born. However, she did not stay in Rome long enough. There was also a holy virgin who gave this creature her meal on Wednesdays. On those other days when she was not provided for, she begged her food from door to door.

*

Another time, just as she came by the house of a poor woman, the poor woman called her into her house and sat her down by her little fire, giving her wine in a stone cup to drink. And she had a baby boy suckling from her breast, whom she breast-fed for a while. At another time he ran to this creature whilst his mother sat full of sorrow and sadness. Then this creature burst into tears as though she had seen our Lady and her son at the time of his Passion, and she had so many holy thoughts that she might never tell the half of them, but continued to sit and weep copiously for a long time, so that the poor woman, not knowing why she wept, took pity on her weeping and begged her to stop.

Then our Lord Jesus Christ said to this creature, 'This place is holy.' And then she got up and went about in Rome and witnessed much poverty among the people. And then she thanked God highly for the poverty she was in, trusting that it would allow her to be partner in merit with them.

Then there was a great gentlewoman in Rome who begged this creature to be godmother to her child whom she named after Saint Bridget, for they had known her in her lifetime. And so she agreed.

---

[27] The Middle English text refers to 'bolendinys', i.e. the Bolognan coins in use in Rome during the fifteenth century.

Afterwards, God gave her grace to receive much love in Rome, both from men and women, and to receive much favour among the people. When the Master and the Brothers of the Hospital of Saint Thomas (who had refused her on a previous occasion, as has been written about before),[28] heard about the love and favour which she had in the city, they entreated her to visit them again, telling her she would be made more welcome than ever she had been before, for they were very sorry that they had put her out from them. And she thanked them for their charity and did as they commanded. And when she had come back to them, they made her very welcome and were very glad that she had come.

Then she found there the girl who had been her maidservant previously,[29] and who should still have been so by right. She was living in the Hospital in much wealth and prosperity, for she was in charge of their wine supply. And sometimes out of humility this creature went to her to ask of her food and drink, and the maid gave it to her willingly and sometimes added to it a groat. Then she complained to her maidservant, saying that she felt great sorrow for her departure, and telling of the great slander and evil words that people uttered because of their separation. However, the maid never wanted to be with her again.

Afterwards, this creature spoke with Saint Bridget's maid in Rome,[30] but she was unable to understand what she said. Then she procured a man who could understand her language and he told Saint Bridget's maid what this creature said, and how she asked after Saint Bridget, her mistress. Then the maid said that her lady, Saint Bridget, was kind and meek to everybody and that she had a laughing face. And also, the good man at this creature's lodgings told her that he knew the saint himself, but that he had not known that she was so holy a woman as she was, for she was always homely and kind to all who wanted to speak with her.

---

[28] This refers to the Hospital of Saint Thomas of Canterbury at Rome which had been established for English pilgrims. Earlier in the narrative Margery has told of how she was well received at the Hospital at first, but was eventually evicted because of the slander of an English priest who had taken exception to her.

[29] This is the same maidservant who is removed from Margery's company whilst at Constance on her way to Jerusalem. See p. 61 above.

[30] Saint Bridget is known to have had three maidservants with her during her own pilgrimage to Jerusalem in 1371. It is likely that this maid belonged to that period of Bridget's life.

She was in the chamber in which Saint Bridget died,[31] and she heard a German priest preaching of her and her revelations and her way of life in that place. And she also knelt on the stone on which our Lord appeared to Saint Bridget and told her the day she should die on.[32] And the day that this creature was in her chapel – which had formerly been the chamber in which she died – was one of Saint Bridget's days.[33]

Summons by the Abbess of Denny [*Book*, pp. 202–3]
In her mature years, Margery seems to have gained enough authority to be actively sought out by others as a source of spiritual comfort and inspiration.

The Abbess of Denny, a house of nuns, often sent for the said creature to come to speak with her and with her sisters.[34] The creature thought she would not go until another year, for she could ill endure the effort. Then, as she was in her meditation and had great sweetness and devotion, our Lord commanded her to go to Denny and comfort the ladies who desired to converse with her, speaking to her soul in this manner: 'Daughter, set out for the house of Denny in the name of Jesus, for I wish you to comfort them.'

She was reluctant to go, for it was a time of pestilence and she thought she would not have died there to any advantage. Our Lord said to her mind again, 'Daughter, you shall go there safely and come back again safely.'

Then she went to a worthy burgess's wife who loved her and trusted her very much, whose husband lay very ill, and she told the worthy wife that she would be going to Denny. The worthy woman did not want her to go. 'I do not wish my husband to die whilst you are away, for forty shillings', she said.

And she replied, 'If you were to give me a hundred pounds I would not stay at home.' For when she was commanded in her soul to go,

---

31 The site of Bridget's home in Rome is now occupied by the Church of Santa Brigida in the Piazza Farnese and was close to the Hospital of Saint Thomas.

32 This revelation occurred five days before Bridget's death.

33 There were three days dedicated to the memory of Saint Bridget: 28th May, 23rd July, and 7th October (now the 8th). It is likely from internal evidence that the day referred to here was that of 7th October, 1414.

34 This was a house situated at Waterbeach on the river Cam, five miles from Cambridge. The nuns here exercised strict enclosure and visitors were generally subject to formal – even papal – permissions. This suggests that Margery's authority as holy woman was now recognised, at least in the local vicinity.

she would in no way withstand it, but for anything she would set off whatever happened. And when she was commanded to be at home, she would not go out for anything.

And then our Lord informed her that the said burgess would not die, and she went back to the worthy wife and told her to be well comforted, for her husband would live and prosper very well and that he would not die yet. The good wife was very glad and replied to her, 'As it has come from your mouth, it must now be Gospel!'

Then this creature would have hurried off as she was commanded, but when she reached the water's edge, all the boats had gone on towards Cambridge before she arrived. Then she had great distress over how she might fulfil our Lord's command, but soon she was commanded in her soul not to be sorry nor distressed, for she would be looked after well enough and she would travel safely and return again safely. And so it happened, indeed

A Legend in her own Lifetime [*Book*, pp. 243–5]

Following her return from her arduous journey to Germany in her old age, Margery travels on to London where she discovers that she has become legendary in her own lifetime – in this case for her perceived hypocrisy.

From there (i.e. Canterbury) she went to London wearing a canvas cloth – like a garment of sacking – just as she had worn overseas. When she came into London, many people knew her well enough. Because she was not dressed as she would like to have been for lack of money, and desiring to have gone unrecognised until she had secured a loan, she carried a handkerchief in front of her face. In spite of doing so, some dissolute persons, supposing it was Margery Kempe of Lynn,[35] said, so that she might easily hear these words of reproof, 'Ah, you false flesh, you shall eat no good meat.'

Not answering, she passed by as if she had not heard. These words had never been uttered by her, neither of God nor of any good man, even though they were attributed to her, and at many times and in many places she had great reproof because of it. They were invented by the devil, father of lies, favoured, maintained and born from his limbs, and by false, injurious people who were indignant at her virtuous way of life, and who had no power to hinder her except through their false tongues. No man nor woman could ever prove that she said such words, but they always made other liars their authori-

35 This is the only occasion when Margery's surname is used in the *Book*.

ties, saying in excuse of themselves that other people told them so. In this way these false words were invented through the suggestion of the devil.

Some person, or else more than one person, deceived by their spiritual enemy, contrived this tale not long after the conversion of the said creature, saying that whilst she was sitting down to a meal on a fish day at a good man's table, when she was served with various fish such as red herring, good pike and such other, she was supposed to have said, as they reported it, 'Ah, you false flesh, you would now eat red herring, but you shall not have your will.' And thereupon she pushed aside the red herring and ate the good pike. And according to them, she was supposed to have said such other things like this, and it therefore sprang up into a type of proverb against her, so that some people said, 'False flesh, you shall eat no herring.' And some said the words which are written before, and all were false, but yet they were not forgotten; they were repeated in many a place where she was not known.

She went on to a worthy widow's house in London where she was well received and welcomed for our Lord's love, and in many places in London she was highly encouraged in our Lord's name – God reward them all.

There was one worthy woman especially who showed her great charity both with food and drink and the giving of other benefits, in whose home on one occasion she was at a meal with various other persons of various status. She was unknown to them and they to her, and some of them came from the Cardinal's house[36] – so she had been told by others. They had a great feast and got on very well. And when they were making merry, some repeated the words written about before, or others like them, that is to say, 'You false flesh, you shall not eat of this good meat.'

She sat still and suffered for a good while. Each of them bantered with the other, having great sport with the imperfection of the person about whom these words were spoken. When they had fully entertained themselves with these words, she asked them if they had any knowledge of the person who was supposed to have spoken these words.

They said, 'No, indeed, but we have heard it told that there is such

---

[36] Henry Beaufort, nominated Cardinal Priest in 1426. Beaufort was the son of John of Gaunt and brother to Lady Westmorland (and therefore half-brother to Henry IV). See n. 15 above.

a false, dissembling hypocrite in Lynn who speaks such words and who, leaving coarse meats, eats up the most delicious and delectable meats which are brought to the table.'

'Look, sirs,' she said, 'you ought to speak no worse than you know, and yet not as evil as you know. Nevertheless, here you speak worse than you know – may God forgive you for it. For I am that same person to whom these words are attributed, who often suffers great shame and reproof, and I am not guilty in this matter, I take God as witness.'

When they saw her unmoved in this matter, not reproving them at all since she desired her correction to be through the spirit of charity, they were admonished by their own honesty, humbling themselves to make amends.

She spoke boldly and strongly wherever she went in London against swearers, cursers, liars and such other vicious people, against the pompous fashions of both men and women. She did not spare them, she did not flatter them, neither for their gifts nor for their food and drink. Her speaking was of great profit to many people. Therefore, when she went into church to undertake her contemplation, our Lord sent her very high devotion, thanking her that she was not afraid to reprove sin in his name and that she suffered scorn and reproof for his sake, promising her very much grace in this life, and after this life to have joy and bliss without end.

She was so comforted in the sweet communing with our Lord that she could not control herself nor rule her spirit according to her own will or according to the discretion of other people, but according to how our Lord would lead it and govern it himself with very bois-terous sobbing and very plentiful weeping. For this reason she suffered very much slander and reproof, especially at the hands of the curates and priests of the churches in London. They would not allow her to remain in their churches, and for this reason she went from one church to another so that she should not be tiresome to them. Many of the common people glorified God in her, having good trust that it was the goodness of God which wrought that high grace in her soul.

Coming to Writing and Collaborating with the Scribe [*Book*, pp. 3–5; 216–20]

[I]t was twenty years and more from that time when this creature first had feelings and revelations before she began to undertake any writing. Afterwards, when it pleased our Lord, he commanded and ordered her that she should undertake the writing of her feelings and revelations and the way of her life so that his goodness might be known to all the world.

Then the creature had no writer who would carry out her desire nor give any credence to her feelings until the time that a man who lived in Germany – he was an Englishman by birth and had since married in Germany and had there both a wife and a child – who knew this creature and her desire well was moved, I trust, by the Holy Ghost and came to England with his wife and his belongings and lived with the said creature until he had written as much as she would tell him during the time that they were together. And after this he died.

Then there was a priest held in great affection by this creature, and so she confided this matter to him and brought him the book to read. The book was so badly written that he could make little sense of it, for it was neither written in good English nor German, nor were the letters shaped or formed as other letters are. Therefore the priest fully believed that nobody would ever be able to read it, except if it were by special grace. Nevertheless, he promised her that if he could read it he would copy it out willingly and write it better.

Then there was such evil talk about this creature and of her weeping that out of cowardice the priest dared but seldom to speak with her, nor would he write as he had promised the said creature. And so he avoided and deferred the writing of this book for nearly four years or more in spite of this creature often entreating him about it. At last, he said to her that he could not read it, for which reason he would not do it. He would not, he said, put himself in danger because of it.

Then he advised her to go to a good man who had been very conversant with the one who first wrote the book, supposing that he would best know how to read the book, for he had sometimes read letters sent from overseas in the other man's handwriting whilst he was in Germany. And so she went to that man, entreating him to write this book and never to reveal it as long as she lived, granting him a great sum of money for his labour. And this good man wrote about a leaf, and yet it was little to the purpose because he could not get on well with it – the book was so badly set out and written so unreasonably.

Then the priest was troubled in his conscience, for he had promised her that he would write this book if he could manage to read it, and he had not carried out his part as well as he night have done; so he asked this creature to get the book back again, if she might kindly do so.

Then she retrieved the book and brought it to the priest very cheer-fully, entreating him to do it with good will, and telling him she would pray to God for him and purchase grace for him to read it and write it also. Trusting in her prayers, the priest began to read this book, and it was much easier, or so he thought, than it had been before. And so he read every word of it over to this creature, and she sometimes helped him where there was any difficulty.

This book is not written in order, everything after another as it happened, but just as the matter came to the creature's mind when it was to be written down. For it was so long before it was written down that she had forgotten the time and the order when things happened. And therefore she wrote nothing but that which she knew very well to be the truth indeed.

*

When this book was first being written, the said creature was more at home in her chamber with the priest doing the writing and said fewer beads than she had done for years before in order to hasten the writing. And when she came to church to hear mass, intending to say her Matins and other such devotions as she had been accustomed to do before, her heart was drawn away from the saying of them and much set upon meditation. Since she was afraid of displeasing our Lord, he said to her soul, 'Do not be afraid, daughter, for as many beads as you would wish to say, I accept them as if you said them; and the dedication with which you have striven to get written the grace that I have shown to you pleases me very much, as does he who is doing the writing too. For even if you were in church and both of you wept together as bitterly as ever you have done, yet you would not please me more than you do with your writing. For, daughter, by this book many people will be converted to me and believe in me.'

*

Here ends this treatise, for God took to his mercy the one who wrote down the copy of this book. And although he did not write clearly or lucidly to our manner of speaking, in his own manner of writing and spelling he made true sense, which – through God's help and that of herself who experienced all of this treatise in feeling and behaviour – is truly drawn out of that copy into the production of this little book.

Interpretive Essay

'wonderfully turnyng & wrestyng hir body':
Agonies, Ecstasies, and Gendered Performances in
The Book of Margery Kempe

I

On one notable occasion in *The Book of Margery Kempe*, Margery's priestly amanuensis interpolates an account of a period of personal scepticism about the author's prophetic abilities, confessing to having repeatedly called upon her to prove to him her own prophetic gifts. He recalls rather shamefacedly that his determined coercion of Margery on this matter was effected by his resolute refusal to continue writing down her text unless she complied with his demands. In view of the many difficulties which Margery has already encountered in finding a suitable amanuensis, she is loath to lose his services and as a consequence she is forced to perform a type of prophecy-on-demand for him. As a result of these prophetic games, which serve to prove to this priest that the word of God can indeed be made manifest in the voice of the woman, the priest is suitably impressed, telling us:

> And so [. . .] this creature did as he entreated her and told him her feelings about what should happen in such matters as he asked her about, to discover whether her feelings were true. And in this way he tested them for their truth. (76)

Taking full credit for validating this prophetic manifestation of the divine word, this priest continues a tradition of compulsory endorsement of the female text by the stamp of male authority.[1] This incident, although ostensibly told against the priest's own scepticism, therefore stands as a paradigm for the difficulties faced by the woman writer – and Margery Kempe in particular – in achieving a

---

1 The doctrine of *discretio spiritum*, as devised to help the priesthood differentiate between divine and diabolic manifestations, has been comprehensively examined in the context of medieval holy women in Rosalyn Voaden, *God's Words, Women's Voices: The Discernment of Spirits in the Writing of Late-Medieval Women Visionaries* (York, 1999).

measure of personal authority, even within her own text. Here, as elsewhere, we are reminded that, even if the impulse towards writing is the woman's own, the ultimate achievement of that design remains dependent on the good-will and endorsement of suitable male authority.

It will therefore come as no surprise that much of *The Book of Margery Kempe* is preoccupied with its protagonist's direct confrontations with such male authorities who are frequently intent on frustrating her desire to be recognised by them as the singular prophetic holy woman, redeemed neo-virgin, and transcendent spouse to the Godhead which she considers herself to be.[2] Similarly, much of Margery Kempe's authorial concern is characterised by a search for authority; as a self-confessed illiterate woman from the mercantile milieu of fifteenth-century Bishop's Lynn, such literary authority, of course, had to be achieved by means other than the traditional route of Latinate learning available to her male contemporaries.[3] Indeed, there has long been a consensus amongst critics that even the type of fragile textual authority forged by her female literary precursors such as Bridget of Sweden and Catherine of Siena, for example, largely eludes Margery because of the ambivalent contribution of her own scribe and the impediments posed by the other male authorities with whom she clashes on multiple occasions.[4] For this reason, the

---

[2]   On Margery Kempe's adoption of virginity (and versions of virginity generally in the Middle Ages), see Sarah Salih, *Versions of Virginity in late Medieval England* (Cambridge, 2001). See, in particular, pp. 166–241.

[3]   The extent of Margery Kempe's authority has been the subject of great debate, as demonstrated in the introduction to this volume. Many commentators have denied her the authority which more recent feminist critics have been anxious to recapture for her. For a negative appraisal see, for example, David Hirsch, *The Revelations of Margery Kempe*, Medieval and Renaissance Authors 10 (Leiden, New York, Kobenhavn, Koln, 1988); Ute Stargardt, 'The Beguines of Belgium, the Dominican Nuns of Germany, and Margery Kempe', in J. Heffernan (ed.), *The Popular Literature of Medieval England* (Knoxville, 1985), pp. 277–313; Thomas Coleman, *English Mystics of the Fourteenth Century* (London, 1938). In more recent times, Rosalynn Voaden has also argued for Margery's limited agency because of a failure to forge an identity of Holy Woman along the lines of Saint Bridget, for example. See Voaden, *God's Words, Women's Voices*, op. cit.

[4]   For a comparative study of the achievements of Bridget of Sweden and Margery Kempe, again see Voaden, *God's Words, Women's Voices*. On Bridget's prophetic authority see Claire L. Sahlin, 'Gender and Prophetic Authority in Birgitta of Sweden's *Revelations*', in Jane Chance (ed.), *Gender and Text in the Later Middle Ages* (Gainesville, 1996), pp. 69–95. On Catherine of Siena see Suzanne Noffke (trans.), *Catherine of Siena: The Dialogue* (London, 1980), Introduction, pp. 1–22. For an examination of Catherine of Siena as marginal woman, see

interest which *The Book of Margery Kempe* initially generated tended to categorise Margery as a type of psychic primitive. More recent feminist study, however, has attempted to rescue Kempe and her *Book* from this delimiting realm and to establish her as an important example of a holy woman and author seeking and gaining a measure of empowerment within a patriarchal socio-religious milieu intent on denying it to her.[5]

This essay will therefore seek to add to the debate surrounding the crucial question of Margery Kempe's agency as woman and as author, and will address the aspect of her subjectivity which has proved to be most problematic to critics in recent times – her mystical ecstasies, or, as those more sceptical of her modern critics would prefer to have it, her 'hysteria'.[6] Taking up a stance which refutes lack of agency and authority, I read both Margery Kempe's life and her work as supremely crafted, and suggest that the author, in her attempt to achieve authority, is in fact skilfully manipulative of the patriarchal preconceptions and prejudices of her audience. I will suggest that by means of an hyperbolised (exaggerated) and largely mimetic adherence to contemporary socio-religious attitudes towards motherhood and female sexuality in particular,[7] Margery Kempe succeeds in subverting their hegemonic restrictions, and is able to

Thomas Luango, 'Catherine of Siena: Rewriting Female Holy Authority', in Lesley Smith and Jane Taylor (eds), *Women, the Book, and the Godly* (Cambridge, 1995), pp. 89–111.

5   The most influential studies of this type are Karma Lochrie, *Margery Kempe and Translations of the Flesh* (Philadelphia, 1991); Lynn Staley, *Margery Kempe's Dissenting Fictions* (Pennsylvania, 1984); Hope Phyllis Weissman, 'Margery Kempe in Jerusalem: *Hysterica Compassio* in the Late Middle Ages', in Mary Carruthers and Elizabeth Kirk (eds), *Acts of Interpretation: The Text in its Contexts 700–1600* (Oklahoma, 1982), pp. 201–17; Kathy Lavezzo, 'Sobs and Sighs between Women: The Homoerotics of Compassion', in Louise Fradenburg and Carla Freccero (eds), *Premodern Sexualities* (New York & London, 1996), pp. 175–98; Sarah Beckwith, 'A Very Material Mysticism: The Medieval Mysticism of Margery Kempe', in David Aers (ed.), *Medieval Literature: Criticism, Ideology, and History* (Brighton, 1986), pp. 34–57; Clarissa Atkinson, *Mystic and Pilgrim: The Book and World of Margery Kempe* (Ithaca, 1983); Diane Watt, *Secretaries of God: Women Prophets in Late Medieval and Early Modern England* (Cambridge, 1997).

6   See, for example, David Knowles, *The English Mystical Tradition* (London, 1961), p. 146: 'There existed quite clearly, and from the beginning of her adult life, a large hysterical element in Margery's personality.'

7   The potential of mimesis (that is to say the miming of male discourse by the woman) to provide a disruptive strategy is examined by Luce Irigaray in *Spéculum of the Other Woman*, trans. Gillian C. Gill (Ithaca, 1985). For an

create a space in which her own authority can be established and from which her own voice can be heard. In so doing, I hope to extrapolate more generally some of the ways in which medieval women writers such as Margery were sometimes able to side-step the proscriptions laid down for them by patriarchal ideology and practices whilst apparently conforming to their dictates.

II

In her examination of the mother as part of the substratum of the social order, the French feminist philosopher, Luce Irigaray posits:

> So what is a mother? Someone who makes the stereotypical gestures she is told to make, who has no personal language and who has no identity.[8]

Irigaray's stance on motherhood emerges from a long line of debate upon this highly emotive subject, a debate which is still as pressing today as it appears to have been in the Middle Ages. At the time when Margery was writing, attitudes towards motherhood were frequently coloured by polemic such as that of the third-century commentator Tertullian who saw women not only as 'the gateway of the devil', but also as the perpetual reincarnation of sinful Eve.[9] For Tertullian, spiritual purity could only be achieved by means of total sexual abstinence, and mothers, along with all women, were creatures of danger in the sexual allure they embodied. On the other hand, such extreme antipathy to women was modified somewhat by the highly influential teachings of Saint Paul: although considering women to be fallen and inferior, he nevertheless envisaged for them salvation through childbearing:

> And Adam was not seduced; but the woman, being seduced, was in the transgression. Yet she shall be saved through child bearing; if she continue in faith and love and sanctification with sobriety.[10]

Allied to the popular late-medieval cults of the Virgin and of Saint Anne who presented images of perfect motherhood to which ordi-

---

assessment of its validity as a strategy see Toril Moi, *Sexual/Textual Politics* (London & New York, 1985), pp. 139–43.

8   Luce Irigaray, 'Women-Mothers, the Silent Substratum of the Social Order', in Margaret Whitford (ed.), *The Irigaray Reader* (Oxford, 1991), pp. 46–52 (50).

9   For extracts from the misogynistic writings of Tertullian, see Alcuin Blamires (ed.), *Woman Defamed and Woman Defended: An Anthology of Medieval Texts* (Oxford, 1992), pp. 50–8.

10 I Timothy 2: 15.

nary women could aspire,[11] attitudes towards motherhood were highly ambivalent, as is reflected in much of the literature of the period. Thus, it comes as no surprise that sentiments emerging from both sides of the divide make themselves apparent in the highly dramatic opening of the *Book of Margery Kempe*. Margery begins her narrative with the painful documentation of the extreme physical and psychological suffering which she incurs following her marriage at the age of twenty to the merchant, John Kempe. Within months of this marriage, Margery finds herself pregnant ('as nature would have it' (31)), and is catapulted into a period of protracted suffering brought on in part by this pregnancy, but also by a failure to confess an unexpiated sin which she has been harbouring in her conscience for some time:

> And when she came to the point of uttering that thing which she had concealed for so long, her confessor was a little too hasty and began to reprimand her sharply before she had fully said what she intended to, and so she would say nothing more, for anything he might do.   (31)

As a result of this disastrously abortive attempt to confess her sin, compounded by the overhasty and judgmental authority of her confessor,[12] Margery falls prey to what she identifies as a diabolic possession, but which modern commentators have tended to recognise as a lengthy post-partum psychosis:[13]

---

11 On the development and popularity of the cult of the Virgin Mary see Marina Warner, *Alone of All her Sex: The Myth and Cult of the Virgin Mary* (London, 1990). See also Maurice Hamington, *Hail Mary? The Struggle for Ultimate Womanhood in Catholicism* (London, 1995). For a contemporary feminist appraisal of the unattainability of those ideals of femininity embodied in the figure of the Virgin see Julia Kristeva, '*Stabat Mater*', in Toril Moi (ed.), *The Kristeva Reader* (New York, 1986), pp. 160–86.

12 For an examination of the power relationship between female penitent and her confessor see E. A. Petroff, 'Male Confessors and Female Penitents: Possibilities for Dialogue', in *Body and Soul: Essays on Medieval Women and Mysticism* (Oxford, 1994), pp. 139–60. For another useful article on this hierarchical and often problematic relationship see Janet Dillon, 'Holy Women and their Confessors or Confessors and their Holy Women?' in Rosalynn Voaden (ed.), *Prophets Abroad: The Reception of Continental Holy Women in Late Medieval England* (Cambridge, 1996), pp. 115–40.

13 See, for example, Julia Bolton Holloway, 'Bridget of Sweden's Textual Community in Medieval England', in Sandra J. McEntire (ed.), *Margery Kempe: A Book of Essays* (New York & London), p. 214, and Janet Wilson, 'Margery and Alisoun: Women on Top', in the same volume, p. 227. Maureen Fries goes even further, describing Margery's illness as 'a painful and lengthy postpartum

> [T]his creature went out of her mind and was amazingly
> tormented and troubled with spirits for half a year, eight
> weeks and odd days.
>
> And during this time she thought she saw devils opening
> their mouths which were all alight with burning flames of
> fire, as if they would have swallowed her in; sometimes they
> pawed at her, sometimes threatening her, sometimes pulling
> at her and dragging her about both night and day during the
> said time. (31)

There is much circumstantial evidence presented to us in the *Book* to
suggest that the unexpiated sin which brings about this bout of
madness is of a sexual nature,[14] but it is also clearly bound up with
Margery's violent transition within a short space of time from desirable young woman from a well-respected family in Bishop's Lynn to
wife of the merchant John Kempe and mother of his child. This is
corroborated by the fact that Margery's suffering at this time
continues unabated for just over eight months – almost the same
length of time as a full-term pregnancy – suggesting that she sees it
as an apt punishment to fit the perceived crime. Significantly, this
'crime' will later clearly be identified with what she sees as an
enforced concupiscence as sexually-active wife and mother torn
between the rigid ideology of commentators like Tertullian and the
more liberal approach of Saint Paul. What Margery makes clear,
however, is that both in her childbirth labour, and in her subsequent
struggle with mental and physical collapse, she literally labours to
the point of death; and her use of the ambiguous – and gendered –
term 'laboured' [labowrd] here becomes highly nuanced.[15] The

depression (apparently in its unipolar manic phase)', 'Margery Kempe', in Paul
Szarmarch (ed.), *An Introduction to the Medieval Mystics of Europe* (Albany,
1984), p. 219. For a modern diagnosis of Margery's illness, see Richard Lawes,
'The Madness of Margery Kempe', in Marion Glasscoe (ed.), *The Medieval
Mystical Tradition: Exeter Symposium VI*, Papers read at Charney Manor, July
1999 (Cambridge, 1999), pp. 147–67. Here Lawes, a trained psychiatrist, brings
to bear contemporary scientific knowledge and diagnostic skills upon Margery's
behaviour. See also Mary Hardman Farley, ' "Her Own Creatur": Religion, Feminist Criticism, and the Functional Eccentricity of Margery Kempe', *Exemplaria*
11, 1 (1999), pp. 1–21. Here Farley reads Margery as psychotic but, in common
with others who are keen to diagnose Margery's illness, is unable to overcome
the problem that modern diagnostic criteria are necessarily contaminated by
cultural considerations.
14 See, for example, Margery's abortive attempt at adultery, pp. 55–8 and her strug-
gles with sexual temptation, pp. 65–7.
15 Two of the meanings attributed to this term by the MED are firstly, the physical

depiction of her suffering in terms of a diabolic possession is also represented in similarly gendered terms, focusing as it does on the dangerous female voice and the corrupt and fleshly body from which it emerges:

> She slandered her husband, her friends and her own self; she spoke many a vituperative and sharp word; she knew no virtue nor goodness; she desired all wickedness. Just as the spirits tempted her to say and do, so she said and did. She would have killed herself many a time as they incited her to do and would have been damned with them in hell, in witness of which she bit her own hand so violently that it was evident all her life thereafter. And she also pitilessly tore the skin on her body over her heart with her fingernails, for she had no other implements, and she would have done something worse except she was bound up and restrained with force both day and night so that she could not do as she wanted. (32)

Margery's use of rhetorical hyperbole here leaves us in no doubt that she has absorbed a myriad of contemporary discourses on the sinful and incontinent female body, which promoted its anarchic voice and sexually dissolute subjectivity as providing a fast-track route to damnation. In her uncompromising depiction of specifically female suffering, we are confronted by a woman in despair, writhing and twisting on the bed, obsessively rending the skin on her breasts with her finger-nails in an attempt to release the demons within. As unredeemed and concupiscent woman, Margery attempts to remove this problematic subjectivity which has been thrust upon her by marriage, motherhood, and the masculinist remonstrations of her male confessor following her abortive confession. In short, Margery's violently physical reaction constitutes a self-reflexive protest at the subjectivity which an authoritative and absolutist patriarchy has inscribed upon her body. Read in this way, it also provides a key to an understanding of those later agonies and ecstasies which will form part of Margery's exaggerated performances of femininity, and will comprise part of her central strategy of personal protest and authorisation.

Margery's adoption of such a strategy first becomes clear

---

struggle to give birth to a child, and secondly, sexual intercourse. Other pertinent meanings signify the struggle to understand something, and the struggle to produce a written text.

following her miraculous recovery from her malady which is effected at the hands of Christ who has appeared to her in the depths of her abjection (32). His materialisation at this point in the narrative has the effect of silencing her frenzied voice, stilling her bodily contortions, and of calming her body and her mind. Her resultant tranquillity enables Christ's words of comfort to enter her soul and offer her the potential of an exit-route from her imprisonment. He asks her: 'Daughter, why have you forsaken me when I never forsook you?' (32). Not only does he proceed to offer her the hope of redemption for the sins for which she has so suffered but also provides a means to a physical and spiritual rebirth. Consequently, when Margery demands from John Kempe on his return the keys to the larder – that potent symbol of the female domestic sphere which he has previously removed from her keeping – she presents to both contemporaries and husband a freshly restored appearance of conformity to appropriate wifely and motherly behaviour, telling us, 'After that, this creature performed all her responsibilities wisely and soberly enough' (33).[16] However, as the narrative has just demonstrated in its account of her first encounter with Christ, Margery Kempe is herself – to echo the words of Luce Irigaray – already patently 'elsewhere'[17] and her return to the domestic sphere at this point is therefore far more complex an issue than has generally been appreciated.

Conventional readings, of course, would recognise in this episode an adherence to a traditional narrative cycle of sin, punishment and salvation. I argue, however, that in fact it heralds a central strategy for empowerment which incorporates both exaggerated performance and dramatic mimesis of recognisably gendered codes of conduct which Margery develops in order to forge for herself a measure of physical and spiritual autonomy. Indeed, Margery's re-appropriation of the female gender-roles of compliant wife and mother upon her recovery from illness here can also be usefully read in terms of a Butlerian notion of 'gender performance'. According to gender theorist Judith Butler, gender is a type of performance which is played out

---

16 For the type of duties expected of a wife and mother in Margery's position in the social strata see Martha C. Howell, *Woman, Production and Patriarchy in Late Medieval Cities* (Chicago, 1986), pp. 10–11. See also Eileen Power, *Medieval Women* (Cambridge, 1985), p. 46.

17 On this type of female interiority see Irigaray's essay, 'This Sex which is not One', in Elaine Marks and Isabelle de Courtivron (eds), *New French Feminisms* (New York, London, Toronto, Sydney, Tokyo, 1981), pp. 99–106 (103).

on the surface of the body rather than emanating from what she regards as a non-existent core (or 'ontology').[18] It is therefore an 'act' rather than a naturally occuring phenomenon, is both intentional and performative and as such comprises a 'contingent construction of meaning'.[19] As I shall illustrate, Margery's own performances of gender constitute just such a construction of meaning by means of her own 'stylized repetition' of female-associated acts and gestures which serve to suggest a recognisable gendered identity to those looking on, but which, in fact, points towards a gendered identity that does not exist in any ontological – or 'natural' – capacity. By means of such performances then, Margery is able to assume a whole host of identities to suit the situation and the moment, identities which are performed by her in a way which suggests conformity, whilst in fact still allowing her to remain true to her own desires, her sense of self and her vocation. It is just such an assumed identity which Irigaray also points towards in her question, 'What is a mother?' with which I began this section of the essay, and it is in the cracks which open up between presumed ontology and Margery's exaggerated representation of it that the key to her strategy of disruption lies, as well as the source of her own authority. As Irigaray has also suggested in the context of gender performance:

To play with mimesis is thus, for a woman, to try to recover the place of her exploitation by discourse, without allowing herself to be simply reduced to it. It means to resubmit herself . . . to 'ideas', in particular to ideas about herself, that are elaborated in/by a masculine logic, but so as to make 'visible', by an effect of playful repetition, what was supposed to remain invisible: the cover-up of a possible operation of the feminine in language.[20]

For Irigaray, the gulf between ontology and representation – what woman *is* and what she *appears* within society to be – is bridged by means of a performance of coded gestures, a mimesis of gendered

18 Judith Butler, *Gender Trouble: Feminism and the Subversion of Identity* (New York & London, 1990), p. 136.
19 Ibid., p. 139. Here Butler suggests that gender is a learned performance of certain acts and gestures which are suggestive of masculinity or femininity within a given context. Such a performance of gender thus enables a man or a woman to construct and adhere to the type of gender normality expected of him/her by the society in which he/she lives.
20 Irigaray, 'The Power of Discourse and the Subordination of the Feminine', in Whitford (ed.), *The Irigaray Reader*, pp. 119–32 (124).

practices, which in turn permit the subversion (or, at the very least, disruption) of masculinist ideology or thinking. It is, of course, just such an ideology which has been articulated by Margery's confessor and which has hitherto proved so inadequate to address the specificity of Margery's female experience, as we have seen. It is on this premise then that Margery Kempe can be regarded as embarking upon her own subversive strategy of mimesis and performance in which the specifically female language of her own body is translated into a means of personal empowerment and authority. In other words, by means of repeated performances of gendered codes of behaviour, Margery Kempe opens up an opportunity for the construction of an epistemology of the feminine (that is to say, a female-centred system of knowledge) which is able to disrupt traditional masculinist discourse and offer an alternative route towards spiritual and physical autonomy and authority.

III

Of course, the principal question arising from the notion of a performed and/or hyperbolised expression of gender as strategy is, to echo the words of Toril Moi, does it actually *work*, and if so, how?[21] In response to this question, Moi concludes that it is the political context of such mimesis which is the crucial factor, not the act of mimesis itself.[22] It is also crucial to take into consideration the role played by the body as a type of gendered text and the ways in which that text might be re-appropriated and rewritten to accommodate a shift in personal subjectivity. Margery Kempe, of course, presents us with the ideal subject matter for a consideration of these questions; after all, it only takes a cursory reading of her *Book* to realise that she emerges from its pages as a paradigm of performativity in her search for personal empowerment.

Perhaps the most explicit example of Margerey's systematic re-appropriation of her own bodily experiences as an effective strategy of empowerment is to be found in her adoption of an extraordinary and highly individualistic expression of piety whilst in Jerusalem. Following the birth of her fourteenth child and a mutually agreed vow of chastity with her husband, Margery embarks upon her arduous pilgrimage to the Holy Land, and it is whilst visiting the locations of the Passion that she is first overcome with what is osten-

---

21 Moi addresses this problem in the context of Irigarayan theory in *Sexual/Textual Politics*, p. 140.
22 Ibid., p. 143.

sibly an intense expression of *imitatio Mariae* – a deeply realised identification with and imitation of the Virgin Mary. This violent *imitatio*, characterised by inordinate tears, boisterous sobbings and a lack of bodily control ending in physical collapse, has been the source of much vilification heaped upon Margery both at the hands of her own contemporaries and by modern-day critics.[23] Recent feminist criticism, however, in particular the work of Hope Phyllis Weissman,[24] has recognised in Margery's behaviour here an engagement with those orthodox discourses of Marian maternity which were everywhere apparent in popular late-medieval representations of the Passion;[25] indeed, there is little doubt that Margery is overtly identifying with the maternal suffering of the Virgin Mother in this pivotal episode at Calvary:

> And when they came up onto Mount Calvary, she fell down so that she could neither stand nor kneel, but writhed and twisted with her body, spreading her arms out wide, and she cried with a loud voice as though her heart would burst apart [. . .]
>
> And she had such great compassion and such great pain to see our Lord's pain that she was not able to keep herself from crying and roaring though she should have died for it [. . .] The crying was loud and so amazing that it made the people astonished, unless they had heard it before or else they knew the reason for the crying.   (37)

Were we to decontextualise this extract, however, we might be forgiven for presuming it to comprise part of that earlier account of post-partum bodily suffering and psychological anguish documented by Margery at the start of her text which I have examined previously. Like the travailing mother, Margery's limbs flail about in uncontrollable gestures of relentless pain. Images of the labouring mother are similarly invoked by Margery's crying and screaming, and are also reminiscent of the voice she (mis)used to slander husband, friends and self during her earlier bout of derangement. Examined in this

---

23 For a brief overview of her early contemporary critics see my introduction, pp. 5–11.

24 Weissman, '*Hysterica Compassio*', op. cit.

25 See, for example, the translation of Pseudo-Bonaventure's *Meditationes Vitae Christi* by Robert Manning, *Meditations on the Supper of Our Lord and the Hours of His Passion*, ed. J. Meadows Cowper, EETS o.s. 60 (London: Oxford University Press, 1875). See also the anonymous verse translation, *Meditations on the Life and Passion of Christ*, ed. Charlotte d'Evelyn, EETS o.s. 158 (London, 1921).

way, Margery Kempe's gesturing during this and similar episodes of apparent *imitatio* can, in fact, be read as a dramatic and hyperbolised re-enactment not just of the Virgin's anguish, but also of her *own* earlier maternal sufferings. In effect, she is imitating her own bodily experiences and recontextualising them as a means of documenting and lending authority to her mystical ecstasy. This bodily language of mimetic performance therefore serves to re-inscribe an intensely personal maternal code upon Margery's body which, because of her physical presence in the very places where the similarly suffering Virgin enacted *her* maternal agonies, becomes a newly feminine text which renders comprehensible to her audience the essentially incomprehensible mystical insight present in Margery's soul.

In his seminal study of the use of gesture in the Middle Ages, Jean-Claude Schmitt has suggested that gestures were actually considered to comprise an outer, bodily expression of the inner workings of the soul.[26] Examined in this light, the extraordinary use of bodily gesturing which Margery Kempe displays during this episode and which continues throughout her book, takes on an even greater significance.[27] Not only does it serve to provide evidence for her contemporaries of the workings of the holy spirit in her soul, but because of the maternal codes embodied within it, it also constitutes an authoritative performance of the feminine – and one which is endorsed by the Virgin's own performances of the same role. In addition to this, whilst appearing to adhere to the orthodox concept of the suffering mother, Margery's performance simultaneously hyperbolises it. As a result, this act of elaborate mimesis succeeds in subverting its own cultural construction.

The efficacy of this as a strategy of authorisation becomes even more apparent during those occasions when Margery Kempe is in most danger – in particular her moments of peril whilst undertaking a later pilgrimage to holy sites within the north of England (80–91). On several occasions, for example, she finds herself arrested by the authorities and is subjected to aggressive ecclesiastic examination

---

[26] Jean-Claude Schmitt, 'The Rationale of Gestures in the West: the Third to the Thirteenth Centuries', in Jan Bremmer and Herman Roodenburg (eds), *A Cultural History of Gesture* (Oxford, 1991), pp. 59–70 (60).

[27] For a more detailed and comprehensive account of the various strategies adopted by Margery Kempe see my article 'Spritual Virgin to Virgin Mother: The Confessions of Margery Kempe', *Parergon* n.s. 17, 1 (July 1999), pp. 9–44. See also Liz Herbert McAvoy, 'The Sexual Spirituality of Margery Kempe', in Susannah Chewning (ed.), *Intersections of Religion and Sexuality: The Word Made Flesh* (Ashgate, forthcoming, 2003).

for heresy. As the socially uncategorisable woman – that is to say one who falls dangerously between the categories of virgin and married woman – Margery is considered doubly aberrant, something which is reflected in her being frequently labelled as both heretic and strumpet. However, on such occasions we frequently see Margery re-enacting another type of maternal and wifely performance, and one which is entirely suited to this altered political context. Now she chooses to draw heavily on traditional and domestic discourses of marriage and motherhood, discourses which involve notions of childcare, storytelling, wifely support and unquestioned monogamy. However, having invoked such discourses, Margery then proceeds to project them back upon the patriarchal court in order to disrupt their assumptions about her and, more importantly, to escape with her life. Perhaps the best example of such a strategy in operation lies in Margery's feisty response to the Leicester court's accusations of heresy and sexual incontinence:

> I call upon Lord Jesus Christ as witness [. . .] that I never partook sinfully of any man's body in this world in actual deed, except for my husband's body, to whom I am bound by the law of matrimony and by whom I have born fourteen children. [115]

Here we see Margery deflecting the deeply threatening male antipathy within this court to her perceived heterodoxy by redefining herself as a faithful married woman and as the mother of fourteen children – the finite, physical symbol of a marital fruitfulness fully condoned by Saint Paul and orthodox attitudes within the Church. The subversiveness of this re-inscription of self in adherence to patriarchal socio-religious orthodoxy is, of course, made all the more intense because we, as her secondary audience of readers, are already privy to the fact that she has radically redefined the boundaries of both these gender roles. However, the authority which this performance of orthodoxy creates in this instance permits her to upbraid the mayor, and by implication the entire room of ecclesiastics:

> 'Sir, you are not worthy to be a mayor, and I shall prove it by citing Holy Writ. For our Lord God himself said before he took vengeance on the cities, "I shall come down and see for myself", and yet he knew all things. And that was for no other reason, sir, than to show men such as you that you should not execute any punishments unless you knew beforehand that they are appropriate. But, sir, you have done the contrary to me today, for you have caused me much

shame for something for which I am not guilty. May God
forgive you for it.'   [116]
Quite simply, Margery Kempe's self-representation as embedded
within her vociferous self-justification announces her singularity
whilst simultaneously re-incorporating it within an orthodox tradition of legitimate and well-respected maternity and loyal wifehood.
In this act of self-definition too, Margery publicly allies herself to
that most perfect and approved-of woman, the Virgin Mary, and
creates an authoritative space in which to remonstrate against the
injustice of patriarchal practices. In this way, Margery's bodily
excesses, her hyperbolised mimesis of feminine social codes, allow
her to position herself at the liminal point of intersection between
orthodox socio-religious practices and marginalised aberrancy. This
liminality is again the site of a convenient lacuna (or gap), identified
by Karma Lochrie as the *fissure*,[28] which provides the location of
authority from which the female mystic can speak and be heard. In
Irigarayan terms, it is the location of a 'blind-spot' in patriarchal
thinking, from where the voice of the mystic can disrupt its hegemonic logic and offer up an incontestable logic of the feminine in its
place. Margery, in effect, outplays the Virgin at her own game of
adherence to a rigid construct of ideal femininity, whilst running
counter to it at the same time by means of her *own* hyperbolic and
redefined adherence to its tenets.

IV

Margery's redefinition of the discourses of motherhood and wifehood and her strategic use of gendered performances in the *Book* are,
however, even more adept and subversive than this analysis has so far
suggested. Indeed, just as we saw in the opening sequences of her
text, there is also a strong element of female sexuality embedded
within Margery's public performances of piety – something which
most critics to date have entirely underestimated. In this context,
Margery's bodily performances can be seen as not only engaging
with her lived experiences as a wife and mother, but also in terms of
an uncompromising confrontation with contemporary attitudes
towards vilified female sexuality.

    Attitudes towards female sexuality in the Middle Ages were fairly
consistent.[29] According to religious belief, based upon the concupis-

28 Lochrie, *Translations*, op. cit.
29 On attitudes towards sexuality and sex difference in the Middle Ages, see Joan

cence which Eve released into the world following the Fall, women were sexually dangerous and inherently incontinent. Not only did they have a greater capacity for prolonged sexual activity than men, they also incited lustful thoughts within the more rational male. As a result, it was considered that women needed to be closely policed and permanently controlled. In the immortal words of Isidore, the seventh-century Archbishop of Seville:

> The word 'female' [*femina*] derives from the area of the thighs [*femorum*] where her gender is distinguished from a man's. But some think she is called 'female' [*femina*] through the Greek etymology for 'burning force' [i.e. Greek *fos*] because of the intensity of her desire. For females [*feminas*] are more lustful than males.[30]

It is certainly such a discourse of female lustfulness which Margery Kempe appears to have internalised in her description of her attempts at adulterous liaison with one of her fellow churchgoers early in her marriage. Following this man's attempted seduction of her and his subsequent humiliating rejection when she attempts to comply, Margery inscribes the sin of lechery upon herself telling us: 'She went away completely ashamed and confused in herself, seeing his steadfastness and her own instability' (57). Similarly, Margery tells us on numerable occasions that sex with her husband had become abominable to her in spite of an earlier delight in sexual activity with him.[31] In fact, as the *Book* progresses, Margery increasingly attempts to eschew her own sexuality in favour of a type of neo-virginity – something she appropriates upon the vow of chastity she extracts from her husband.

Yet, when we come to examine Margery's performances more closely it is possible to uncover a strong discourse of sexuality permeating them at every juncture. Indeed, it is possible to assert that Margery's earlier sexual experiences become as much an intrinsic part of her mimetic performances as are her experiences of motherhood and wifehood. This time, however, rather than being achieved by means of an *imitatio Mariae*, Margery's identification is with the

---

Cadden, *Meanings of Sex Difference in the Middle Ages: Medicine, Science and Culture* (Cambridge, 1993).
[30] Isidore of Seville, *Etymologies* xi. Ii. 24, as cited in Blamires (ed.), *Women Defamed*, p. 43.
[31] See, for example, p. 55.

orthodox – and yet wholly redeemed – fallen woman, Mary Magdalene, from whom she draws further authority.[32]

In this context, it is highly significant that Margery chooses to ground her entire narrative in the authority offered by this former prostitute and saint, telling us at the onset that the task of writing was begun 'on the day of our Lord 1436, on the day following Mary Magdalene's day' [6], and references to this so-called 'harlot saint' everywhere abound in the narrative. Recounting her travels in Jerusalem, for example, Margery tells us explicitly: 'she (Margery) stood in the same place as Mary Magdalene stood when Christ said to her, "Mary, why are you weeping?" ' (41). It is clear here that Margery is most keen to associate her own weeping at Calvary not only with the maternal weeping of the Virgin, but also with the traditional tears of abjection of the redeemed prostitute, Mary Magdalene. Indeed, during this entire sequence Margery's identification with the Magdalene, which has been incipient since the onset of her narrative, becomes increasingly insistent. Even the Virgin herself at this point draws an explicit comparison between her own tears, the tears of Margery and those of the Magdalene:

[D]o not be ashamed of him who is your God, your Lord and your love, any more than I was to cry and to weep for the pain of my sweet son, Jesus Christ, when I saw him hanging on the cross; nor was Mary Magdalene ashamed to cry and weep for my son's love.   (41)

Thus, it becomes evident that Margery is actually superimposing upon her authoritative identification with the Virgin a second narrative in which she conflates herself with the once vilified and sexually dissolute Mary Magdalene.[33] Examined in this context, Margery's excess of tears and grief are therefore simultaneously those of the grieving mother and those of the repentant whore at the moment of *her* apotheosis. In this way Margery overlays her subversive re-enactment of the pains of childbirth with a dramatic performance of vilified female sexual desire which, again like the Magdalene, she can effectively redirect towards the adoration of Christ in this act of legitimisation. In so doing, she rescues her own sexuality from the

32 On Margery Kempe's *imitatio* of Mary Magdalene as represented in the Digby Corpus Christi plays see Suzanne Craymer, 'Margery Kempe's Imitation of Mary Magdalene and the Digby Plays', *Mystics Quarterly* 19 (1993), pp. 173–81. See also my essay, 'The Sexual Spirituality of Margery Kempe', op. cit.

33 Popular representations of Mary Magdalene in the Middle Ages as found in Jacobus de Voragine's *Golden Legend* and in the Digby *Mary Magdalen* play, for example, emphasise her sexual libidinousness and licentiousness.

realm of the abject from where it has been relegated by socio-
religious ideology and utilises it as an experiential tool to further establish her own gynaecentric (female-centred) authority.

Such an assertion can be fully corroborated by reconsidering the
Jerusalem narrative under examination. We now find that the terminology used by Margery to describe her bodily incontinence –
words and phrases such as 'writhed', 'twisted with her body',
'spreading her arms', 'cried out with a loud voice as if her heart
would burst apart' – are all equally as applicable to the spontaneous
gestures invoked by female orgasm as to those of the parturient
(birthing) mother. This reading is further reinforced by Margery's
embellishment of her passionate response at Calvary – details which
again further invoke the bodily contortions and articulations of
female sexual ecstasy:

And when her body might no longer endure the spiritual
exertion but was overcome with the unspeakable love which
worked so fervently in her soul, then she fell down and cried
amazingly loud. And the more she struggled to keep it in or
to suppress it, so much the more would she cry, and even
louder. (38)

Margery is also emphatic that 'these bodily contortions (were) a
result of the fire of love which burnt so passionately in her soul' (38),
a fire which she also explicitly alludes to during her moments of
mystical union with Christ himself during her later mystical ecstasies.[34] Thus, it becomes quite clear that Margery's response to her
mystical insights at Calvary is being informed not merely by traditional and orthodox mystical terminology connected with flames of
fire as utilised by Richard Rolle, for example, or indeed by the erotic
imagery contained within the popular Song of Songs, but by her own
recently relinquished sexual experiences. In the same way as she
redeploys the gendered codes of childbirth to authorise her unique
comprehension of the Passion, so now we can also detect an inscription of female desire which is based on her own corporeal and
emotional experiences of sexual satisfaction. Such a highly visible
public performance of female sexual ecstasy, therefore, simultaneously engages with contemporary socio-religious attitudes
towards the incontinent female body, but, by means of a skilful
recontextualisation, presents them in a way which is wholly orthodox

---

[34] See, for example, p. 73. It is likely that such imagery has been borrowed from
that of Richard Rolle whose *Incendium Amoris* [Fire of Love] Margery has told
us she is familiar with (see p. 95).

because of the tradition of mystical metaphor into which they fall and because of the Magdalene-like route to salvation which they can provide for the female sinner. In addition, as a result of this redefined performance of sinful female sexuality Margery Kempe succeeds in interrogating the validity of misogynistic attitudes towards female desire and in challenging their hegemony. In so doing, she ultimately promotes its excess – or in Irigarayan terms, its *jouissance* – (and by implication her own experience of it) as a primary means of by-passing male authority and directly accessing the divine.[35]

V

Much of twentieth- and twenty-first century criticism of Margery Kempe since the rediscovery of her *Book* in 1934 has entirely ignored these insistent discourses which permeate this challenging text, preferring instead to focus on what they consider to be the 'hysterical' tendencies of its protagonist.[36] Like many of her less tolerant contemporaries, modern critics too have been guilty of responding to Margery Kempe as a woman who is out of control – whether the control of a patriarchal society or, indeed, her own self-control. The implication has been that Margery Kempe's extraordinary life and experiences were the result of some kind of psychological disturbance, repressed sexuality even, which re-emerged in a type of aberrant and anti-social behaviour classified as hysteria, with all the negative associations attached to that term. In the light of the argument put forward in this essay, however, it is now possible to reclaim the term as one which encapsulates perfectly the multifaceted strategy of empowerment contained within Margery Kempe's redefinition of both maternity and female desire.

One modern commentator who has done much to transform our perception of Margery Kemp's behaviour – and her hysteria – is Hope Phyllis Weissman whose primary contribution has been to rescue the term 'hysteria' from the realms of negativity by seizing on

35 Irigaray uses the word *jouissance* to represent a female sexual pleasure which lies outside what she refers to as the 'phallic model' (that is to say the male way of defining it). Instead, *jouissance* refers to the satisfying of a specifically *female* sexual desire ('excess') which is in harmony with female identity. For Irigaray, *jouissance* can only be achieved by a woman's rediscovery of both her *own* desire and her *own* identity rather than the desire and identity which men impose upon her.

36 See Introduction, p. 8, n. 17.

its etymology (linguistic origins) and re-using it in its literal capacity as 'womb-suffering'.[37] According to Weissman, as a womb-suffering mother, Margery Kempe displays a 'womb-to-womb' empathy with the Virgin at Calvary in a display of suffering based on an experiential maternal projection and identification, something I have already examined. Whilst this interpretation is undoubtedly highly valid, as I have illustrated, in the light of my own argument we can now add to this assessment by asserting that Margery also engages in a type of womb-to-womb identification with Mary Magdalene and her sexual persona which produces the same agonistic and ecstatic responses in Margery as those produced in the context of maternity. Indeed, if we turn for a moment to some of the discussions of female sexuality as contained within contemporary medical and anatomical treatises, we can recognise their re-emergence within depictions of Margery's 'womb-suffering' in her text. Although we have no evidence to suggest that Margery Kempe had ever read such treatises, or even had them read to her, the many occasions on which she records her successful ministering to sick and suffering women, sometimes even in a gynaecological capacity,[38] would suggest that she was not entirely ignorant of contemporary scientific discourses on the female body. In addition, Monica Green has comprehensively demonstrated the widespread popularity of vernacular treatments of the so-called *Trotula* texts in the late Middle Ages,[39] and translations into the English vernacular of other popular treatises by medical practitioners such as Henri de Mondeville, for example, would testify to a new accessibility to such literary corroboration of the commonly held beliefs about the physiology of the female body. There is also evidence to suggest that Margery's contemporary, Julian of Norwich, with whom she spent several days in conversation in 1413, was also

---

37 Weissman, '*Hysterica Passio*'. Hysteria was originally considered to be an 'ailment' which was exclusive to the female as a result of uterine disorder.

38 See, for example, pp. 52–3. On another occasion, whilst in Rome, Margery visits a woman who is breast-feeding a small child and who is given to fits of melancholy (p. 96). Elsewhere, she is given leave to kiss female lepers [176], and again, whilst in Italy, she cares protractedly for an old woman who is sick, [85–6].

39 Monica H. Green, 'Obstetrical and Gynecological Texts in Middle English', in *Women's Healthcare in the Medieval West: Texts and Contexts* (Aldershot, Burlington, Singapore, Sidney, 2000), pp. 53–88. This essay first appeared in *Studies in the Age of Chaucer* 14 (1992), pp. 53–88. See also Green, 'The Development of the *Trotula*', *Women's Healthcare*, pp. 199–203. This essay was first published in *Revue d'Histoire de Textes* 26 (1996), pp. 119–203.

familiar with such texts and drew upon them in her own writing.[40]
One highly popular medical text written by Gilbertus Anglicus, for
example, focuses intently on the myriad of gynaecological problems
to which woman could be subject,[41] and to this writer woman was
regarded as the reification of her own dysfunctional physiology: as
he tells us 'id est matrix', woman *is* her womb.[42] For the writer of this
text, woman and her problematic womb were indistinguishable and,
indeed, according to Platonic ideology still prevalent in the late
Middle Ages, an unsatisfied and autonomous womb could even
express its desire for sexual intercourse and childbearing by wandering insatiably around the female body which housed it.[43] On occasions, and particularly during periods of severe deprivation, it might
even become lodged in the throat, in which case it would cause the
woman to display symptoms of breathlessness, choking, screaming,
lack of bodily control and extreme pallor, possibly leading to physical collapse.[44] According to Plato's *Timaeus*, a text which remained
highly popular in the late Middle Ages:

> [I]n women [. . .] what is called the matrix or womb, a living
> creature within them with a desire for child-bearing, if it be
> left long unfruitful beyond the due season, is vexed and
> aggrieved, and wandering throughout the body and blocking
> the channels of the breath, by forbidding respiration, brings
> the sufferer to extreme distress and causes all manner of
> disorders; until at last the Eros of the one (the male) and the
> Desire of the other bring the pair together.[45]

Only frequent sex leading to regular childbearing, it would seem,
could restrain this monstrous organ and thus normalise female behaviour. Read in the context of Margery's behaviour in Jerusalem,
we can perhaps see the ways in which this popularly held belief
appears to have been informing her own performances. Read also in
the light of Weissman's theory of 'womb-suffering', it is possible to

---

40 On Julian's use of medical discourses see Alexandra Barratt, ' "In the Lowest
    Part of our Need": Julian and Medieval Gynecological Writing', in Sandra
    McEntire (ed.), *Julian of Norwich: A Book of Essays* (New York & London,
    1998), pp. 240–56.
41 Green, 'Obstetrical and Gynecological Texts', pp. 73–5.
42 Ibid, p. 74.
43 On this see Cadden, *Meanings of Sex Difference*, p. 15.
44 My thanks to J. A. Tasioulas for pointing out the possibility of there being a
    connection between this belief and Margery Kempe's expressions of piety.
45 Francis Macdonald Cornford (trans.), *Plato's Cosmology: the Timaeus of Plato*
    (London, 1937), p. 357.

uncover how these performances of the orthodox served to undermine their own hegemony by reasserting themselves as a text announcing divine privilege. Like Mary Magdalene and the Virgin before her, Margery's exploitation of her own experiential 'womb-suffering' serves ultimately to redeem the vilified female body and offer the feminine as an alternative route to salvation. In effect, Margery's hysteria becomes the site of what Irigaray has recognised more recently as the voice which has been repressed by masculine discourse:

> Hysteria is silent and at the same time it mimes. And – how could it be otherwise – miming/reproducing a language that is not its own, masculine language, it caricatures and deforms that language: it 'lies', it 'deceives', as women have always been reputed to do.[46]

In this way, if hysteria is the display of all that has been silenced by woman's requirement to enter into a mimesis of what is demanded of her by patriarchal ideology, if it constitutes a gesturing which represents the (still silent) language of woman's forbidden self, Margery Kempe's own habitual use of 'hysterical' behaviour can be seen as deeply subversive and empowering, defeating as it does the limitations of its own defining characteristics. It becomes the insistent utterance of the repressed 'voices' of maternity and female sexuality which would otherwise have had to remain in their policed locations of containment. Ultimately, then, it is a redefined and recontextualised notion of hysteria which enables such specifically feminine discourses to be heard and their place within theological and/or mystical discourse to be asserted. Now Margery Kempe's 'hysteria' is transformed by hyperbolic re-enactment not merely into a mystically realised *imitatio* of those most sanctified role models, the Virgin and Mary Magdalene, but also constitutes an alternative – and specifically female – vessel from which the salvific word/Word of God may emerge. As a result, far from excluding her from access to the sacred text, Margery's female body becomes the embodiment of that text itself, and the vilified female is thus transformed into the ultimate expression of holiness and grace.

Finally, it is her highly self-conscious performances of gender which also allow for the dissemination of the holy text to her audiences. In this way, such performances serve to create a screen behind which Margery can operate in order to achieve authority both as holy

---

46 Irigaray, 'Questions', in Whitford (ed.), *The Irigaray Reader*, pp. 133–9 (138).

woman and author; in turn this provides her with a voice which emerges from its location of repression and which will proceed to express the hitherto inexpressible. In short, as well as being the location of a 'blind spot' within the eye of the patriarchy which is always vulnerable to exploitation, it also serves to render Margery Kempe, both in her life and in her text, simultaneously and insistently present, but always and already entirely 'elsewhere'.

Appendix

Printed Extracts from *The Book of Margery Kempe*[1] (from the print of Wynkyn de Worde (1501))

Here begins a short treatise on contemplation as taught by our Lord Jesus Christ, or taken out of the book of Margery Kempe of Lynn.[2]
She desired many times that her head might be severed with an axe upon a block for the love of our Lord Jesus.

Then our Lord Jesus said to her in her mind, 'I thank you, daughter, that you would die for my love, for as often as you think it, so you shall receive the same reward in heaven as if you had suffered that same death, and yet no man shall put you to death.' [30]

'I assure you in your mind that if it were possible for me to suffer pain again as I have done before, I would prefer to suffer as much pain as ever I did for your soul alone, rather than that you should leave me forever.' [30]

'Daughter, you may please God in no better way than to think continually of his love.'

Then she asked our Lord Jesus Christ how she should best love him. (34 [49])

And our Lord said, 'Be mindful of your own wickedness and think about my goodness.' (34 [49])

'Daughter, if you wore your coat of mail[3] or your hair shirt, fasting on bread and water, and even if you were to say a thousand *Our Fathers* every day, you should not please me as well as you do when you are in silence and allow me to speak to you in your soul.' (73 [89])

---

1 As before, page references for these extracts within the Middle English text are included in square brackets and refer to the Meech and Allen edition. Numbers in round brackets refer to the location of the extracts in this present volume.

2 A later edition of this redaction was printed by Henry Pepwell in 1521. That edition inserts the designation 'anchoress' (ancresse) immediately after Margery's name at this point.

3 See p. 73, n. 12.

'Daughter, to say many beads[4] is good for those who can do no better, and yet it is not profitable.[5] But it is a good route towards perfection. For I tell you, daughter, those who are great fasters and penitents want that to be considered the best way of life. And those who give themselves to many devotions want that to be considered the best way of life. And those who donate many alms, they want that to be held the best way of life. And I have often told you, daughter, that meditation, weeping and high contemplation is the best life on earth, and you will have more merit in heaven for one year of thinking in your mind than for a hundred years of praying with your mouth, and yet you will not believe me for you will say many beads.' (74 [89])

'Daughter, if you knew how sweet your love is to me, you would never do anything but love me with all your heart.' [157]

'Daughter, if you want to be high in heaven with me, keep me always in your mind as much as you may and do not forget me at mealtimes, but think always that I sit in your heart and know every thought that is in there, both good and bad.' [184]

'Daughter, I have suffered many pains for your love; therefore you have good reason to love me very well, for I have bought your love most dearly.' (48 [190–1])

'Dear Lord, I pray you, let me never have any other joy on earth but mourning and crying for your love; for I think, Lord, even if I were in hell, if I could weep and mourn there for your love as I do here, hell should not vex me, but it would be a type of heaven – for your love puts away all kinds of fear of our spiritual enemy. For I would rather be there as long as you wanted me to be and to please you, than to be in this world and displease you. Therefore, good Lord, as you desire, so may things be.' [215–16]

She had great wonder that our Lord would become man and suffer such grievous pains for her who was so unkind a creature to him. And then with great weeping she asked our Lord Jesus how she might best please him. And he answered her in her soul, saying, 'Daughter, keep in mind your own wickedness and think of my goodness.'

Then she prayed these words many times: 'Lord, for your good-

---

4   See p. 74, n. 14.
5   'Profyte'. The variant of this word in Pepwell's version reads 'perfyte', and the original text of the *Book* renders it 'parfyte'. It would appear that the use of the word 'profyte' in the de Worde redaction here can be attributed to erroneous reading or transcription by the original redactor or his scribe.

ness, have mercy upon my great wickedness, as certainly as I was never so wicked as you are good, nor may I ever be, even though I would want to; for you are so good that you may be no better. Therefore it is a great wonder that anybody should be parted from you without end.' [207–8]

When she saw the crucifix, or if she saw a man or animal had a wound, or if a man beat a child in front of her, or whipped a horse or any other animal, if she were to see or hear it, she thought she saw our Lord being beaten or wounded just as she witnessed it in the man or the animal. (37 [69])

The more she increased in love and devotion, the more she increased in sorrow and contrition, in humbleness and meekness and in holy dread of our Lord Jesus, and in the knowledge of her own frailty. So that if she saw any creature being punished or sharply chastised, she would think that she had been more worthy of chastisement than was that creature because of her unkindness against God. Then she would weep for her own sin and for compassion of that creature. [172]

'In anything that you do or say, daughter, you may not please God better than to believe that he loves you. For if it were possible for me to weep with you, I would weep with you for the compassion which I have for you.' [81–2]

Our merciful Lord Jesus Christ drew this creature into his love and into thinking of his Passion, so that she could not endure to look upon a leper or any other sick man, especially if he had any wounds appearing on him. So she wept as if she had seen our Lord Jesus with his bleeding wounds, and she did so in the sight of her soul. For, through contemplating the sick man, her mind was completely ravished by our Lord Jesus, so that it caused her great mourning and sorrowing that she could not kiss lepers when she met them in the street, for the love of our Lord. This was something which was completely contrary to her disposition during the years of her youth and prosperity, for then she abhorred them more than anything. [176–7]

'Daughter, you have desired in your mind to have many priests in the town of Lynn who might sing and read night and day in order to serve, worship and praise me, and to thank me for the good things that I have done to you on earth. Therefore, daughter, I promise you that you shall have return and reward in heaven for your good will and your good desires, as if you had actually done them.' [203–4]

'Daughter, you shall have as great a return and as great a reward with me in heaven for the good service and the good deeds that you have performed in your mind, as if you had performed the same things outwardly with your bodily faculties.' [203]

'And, daughter, I thank you for the charity that you have for all lecherous men and women, for you pray for them and weep for them many a tear in the desire that it[6] will deliver them from sin, and because you are as gracious to them as I was to Mary Magdalene, so that they may have as much grace to love me as did Mary Magdalene – with the condition that you wish that every one of them should have twenty pounds a year to love and praise me. And, daughter, this great charity which you show for them in your prayers pleases me very well. And, daughter, I also thank you for the charity which you show in your prayers when you pray for all Jews and Saracens and all heathen people to come to the Christian faith, so that my name might be magnified in them. Furthermore, daughter, I thank you for the general charity that you have for all people alive in this world and to all those who will be up until the world's end; and because you would be hacked up as small as meat for the pot for the love of them so that I would save them all from damnation by your death, if it pleased me to do so. And therefore, daughter, for all these good wills and desires you shall have full return and reward in heaven – believe it well and never doubt it.' [204]

She said, 'Good Lord, I wish I could be laid naked upon a hurdle[7] for your love, so that all men would wonder at me and throw filth and dirt at me, and I should be driven from town to town every day of my life, if it were pleasing to you and was of hindrance to nobody's soul – may your will be fulfilled and not mine.' [184]

'Daughter, as often as you say or think "Worshipped be all the holy places in Jerusalem in which Christ suffered bitter pain and passion", you shall have the same pardon as if you were there with your bodily presence, both for yourself and for all those to whom you will give it.' [75]

'That same pardon which was granted to you previously was confirmed on Saint Nicholas's Day, that is to say plenary remission; and it is not only granted to you, but also to all who believe – and to

---

6   The original version in the *Book* here reads 'I' instead of 'it', thus attributing the deliverance of sinners from their sin to the powers of Christ rather than to Margery's tears.

7   Used in this context, in Middle English the word 'hurdel' refers to a type of cart to which prisoners were strapped in order to be ferried to the place of execution.

all of those who will believe until the world's end – that God loves you, and to whoever will thank God for you. If they will forsake their sin and fully intend never to turn to it again, but are sorry and heavy for what they have done and will undertake due penance for it, they shall have the same pardon that is granted to you yourself, and that is all the pardon that is in Jerusalem, as was granted to you at Ramleh.' [175–6][8]

On that day when she suffered no tribulation for our Lord's sake she was not happy or glad as she was on the day when she suffered tribulation. [120]

'Patience is worth more than the performing of miracles.' [121]

'Daughter, it gives me more pleasure that you suffer humiliation, scorn, shame and reproof, wrongs and diseases, than if your head were struck three times a day every day for seven years.' [131]

'Lord, for your great pain, have mercy on my little pain.' [137]

When she was in great trouble, our Lord said, 'Daughter, I must comfort you. For now you have found the right way to heaven. This is the way I came myself, as did all my disciples. For now you shall know all the better what sorrow and shame I suffered for your love, and you shall have all the more compassion when you think about my Passion.' [156]

'Oh, my dearly esteemed Lord: you should show these graces to religious men and to priests.' [158]

Our Lord replied to her, 'No, no, daughter, for that which I love best, they do not love best, namely shame, reproofs, scorn and humiliation at the hands of the people, and therefore they shall not have this grace. For, daughter, he who fears the shame of the world may not perfectly love God.' [158]

Here ends a short treatise called Margery Kempe of Lynn, imprinted in Fleet Street by Wynkyn de Worde.[9]

---

8 Ramleh (referred to in the *Book* as 'Rafnys') was about a dozen miles from Jaffa, the port at which the pilgrims disembarked for Jerusalem. Margery and her fellow pilgrims stay here on their way back to Jaffa from Jerusalem and prior to embarking on their journey by sea back to Venice. It is here that Christ reassures Margery that just by meditating on the places of the Passion in Jerusalem she will achieve the same pardon as if she were there in body.

9 Again, the later Pepwell edition inserts 'a devoted anchoress' (a deuote ancres) before Margery's name here.

Select Bibliography

Annotated items represent works which may be of particular importance or interest to the reader new to this text. Items which remain unannotated are generally to be considered as providing standard background material.

I. Editions and Translations
Kempe, Margery, *The Book of Margery Kempe*, ed. Sandford Brown Meech and Hope Emily Allen, EETS o.s. 212 (London, New York & Toronto: Oxford University Press, 1997).

This edition remains the most authoritative and exhaustive to date, its editors being amongst the first scholars to engage with the text following its rediscovery in 1934. Modern commentators remain indebted to their meticulous and intensive scholarship.

———, *The Book of Margery Kempe*, trans. Barry Windeatt (Harmondsworth: Penguin, 1985; repr. 1986, 1988).

An accessible and readily available translation with useful, if brief, introduction.

———, *The Book of Margery Kempe*, ed. Barry Windeatt (Harlow: Longman, 2000).

A welcome, more accessible edition which builds upon recent scholarship whilst still indebted to the Meech and Allen edition. Contains on-page glossing and glossary of common words.

———, *The Book of Margery Kempe*, trans. and ed. Lynn Staley, Norton Critical Edition (New York & London: W. W. Norton & Co., 2001).

Another new translation of the text by an authoritative Margery Kempe scholar. Particularly useful to the student in its inclusion of a selection of the most influential and challenging essays on the text to date from a number of different theoretical perspectives, as well as providing useful extracts from contextual primary texts.

II. Other Primary Sources
Barratt, Alexandra, *Women's Writing in Middle English* (Harlow: Longman, 1992).

An accessible and authoritative selection of annotated editions of key medieval female-authored texts. Each text is comprehensively intro-

duced and this book provides an invaluable resource for anyone interested in the writing of medieval women and its historical context.

Birgitta of Sweden, *Saint Bride and her Book: Birgitta of Sweden's Revelations*, ed. & trans. Julia Bolton Holloway (Cambridge: D. S. Brewer, 1992).
A neat and accessible translation most useful to the reader who wishes to investigate the influence of Bridget's writings upon Margery Kempe's own.

———, *The Liber Celestis of St Bridget of Sweden*, ed. Roger Ellis, EETS v. 291 (London, Oxford University Press, 1988).
A somewhat unwieldy edition but fully comprehensive in its notes and introduction.

Blamires, Alcuin (ed.), *Woman Defamed and Woman Defended: An Anthology of Medieval Texts* (Oxford: Oxford University Press, 1992).
An excellent anthology for contextualising commonly held beliefs and attitudes towards women throughout the Middle Ages. A useful teaching resource.

Bokenham, Osbern, *A Legend of Holy Women*, ed. & trans. Sheila Delany (Notre Dame & London: University of Notre Dame Press, 1992).

———, *Legendys of Hooly Wummen* [c. 1447], ed. Mary Serjeantson, EETS o.s. 206 (London: Oxford University Press, 1938).
A user-friendly edition of the Lives of a selection of popular women saints and a lively and entertaining translation.

Catherine of Siena: The Dialogue, trans. Suzanne Noffke (London: SPCK, 1980).
A scholarly and accessible translation of the text with succinct and focused introduction.

Gardner, Edmund D. (ed.), *The Cell of Self-Knowledge: Seven Early English Mystical Treatises Printed by Henry Pepwell in 1521* (London: Chatto & Windus; New York: Duffield, 1910).
Contains an edition of the redacted version of the Book *which was the only version available to scholars before the discovery of the full text in 1934.*

Hamer, Richard and Vida Russell, *Supplementary Lives in Some Manuscripts of the* Gilte Legende, EETS o.s. 315 (Oxford: Oxford University Press, 2000).
A very useful hagiographic resourc, although with limited introductory material. This volume anticipates publication of the main text of the Legende.

Hilton, Walter, *The Ladder of Perfection*, ed. & trans. Leo Sherley-Price (Harmondsworth: Penguin, 1988).
An accessible and readily available translation of this influential text.
Hrosvit of Gandersheim, *Hrosvit of Gandersheim: A Florilegium of her Works*, ed. & trans. Katharina M. Wilson (Cambridge: D. S. Brewer, 1998).
Provides useful and accessible insight into this early Continental mystic.
Hudson, Anne (ed.), *Selections of English Wycliffite Writings* (Cambridge: Cambridge University Press, 1978).
Julian of Norwich, *Revelations of Divine Love*, ed. Frances Beer (Heidelberg: Carl Winter Universitätsverlag, 1978).
Compact and useful scholarly edition of the Sloane 1 manuscript version of the Long Text.
——, *Revelations of Divine Love* and *The Motherhood of God*, ed. & trans. Frances Beer (Cambridge: D.S. Brewer, 1998).
Scholarly edition and translation of the Short Text by a leading Julian authority.
Love, Nicholas, *Mirror of the Blessed Life of Jesus Christ: A Critical Edition Based on Cambridge University Library Additional MSS 6578 and 6686*, ed. M. Sargent (New York: Garland, 1992).
Manning, Robert, *Meditations on the Supper of Our Lord and the Hours of His Passion*, ed. J. Meadows Cowper, EETS o.s. 60, (London: Oxford University Press, 1875).
A work which is useful for contextualising Margery Kempe's displays of affective piety.
Nelson, Venetia (ed.), *A Myrour to Lewde Men and Wymmen: A Prose Version of the 'Speculum Vitae'*, Middle English Texts 14 (Heidelberg: Winter, 1981).
Voragine Jacobus de, *The Golden Legend*, trans. William Granger, 2 vols. (Princeton: Princeton University Press, 1983).
A modern translation of one of the most popular collections of saints' Lives during the Middle Ages and upon which the Gilte Legende *was based (see earlier entry:* Hamer, Richard and Vida Russell (eds), *Supplementary Lives in Some Manuscripts of the* Gilte Legende, *EETS o.s. 315 (Oxford: Oxford University Press, 2000)). Most useful for the reader interested in the hagiographic elements of Margery Kempe's* Book.

III. General Context
Britnell, R. H., *The Commercialisation of English Society, 1000–1500* (Cambridge: Cambridge University Press, 1993).
Provides an overview of the effects of commercial activity on English

society and is helpful for contextualising the urban world in which Margery Kempe was living and operating.

Cadden, Joan, *Meanings of Sex Difference in the Middle Ages: Medicine, Science and Culture* (Cambridge: Cambridge University Press, 1993).
An invaluable book for any student interested in feminist issues or issues of gender in the context of medieval women and their texts.

Coleman, T. W., *English Mystics of the Fourteenth Century* (London: The Epworth Press, 1938).
A now somewhat outdated appraisal of the English mystics. Useful for providing an insight into early twentieth-century attitudes, however.

Duby, George, *Love and Marriage in the Middle Ages* (Chicago: Polity Press, 1994).

Elliott, Dyan, *Spiritual Marriage: Sexual Abstinence in Medieval Wedlock* (Princeton: Princeton University Press, 1993).
An important analysis of the type of sexual imperatives which Margery Kempe identifies in her book. In particular it helps to put in its socio-religious context Margery's desire for sexual abstinence and spiritual union with God.

Hudson, Anne, *The Premature Reformation: Wycliffite Texts and Lollard History* (Oxford & New York: Clarendon, 1988).

Knowles, David, *The English Mystical Tradition* (London: Burns & Oates, 1961).
Useful for an assessment of the progress made within scholarly interest in the English Mystics during the twentieth century.

Ohler, Norbert, *The Medieval Traveller*, trans. Caroline Hillier (Woodbridge: The Boydell Press, 1989).
An informative and accessible book which provides insights into the type of pressures on and motivations of the pilgrim during the Middle Ages.

Riehle, Wolfgang, *Middle English Mystics* (London: Routledge, 1981).
Provides a useful overview of the common literary themes to be found in English mystical writings.

Rubin, Miri, *Corpus Christi: The Eucharist in Late Medieval Culture* (Cambridge: Cambridge University Press, 1991).
An excellent, scholarly study of the implications and resonances surrounding Eucharistic piety at the time when Margery Kempe was operating.

Schmitt, Jean-Claude, 'The Rationale of Gestures in the West: the Third to the Thirteenth Centuries', in Jan Bremmer and Herman

Roodenburg (eds), *A Cultural History of Gesture* (Oxford: Polity Press, 1991).

Stone, Robert K., *Middle English Prose Style* (The Hague & Paris: Mouton, 1970).

Sumption, Jonathan, *Pilgrimage: An Image of Mediaeval Religion* (London: Faber, 1975).

Szarmarch, Paul (ed.), *An Introduction to the Medieval Mystics of Europe* (Albany: State University of New York Press, 1984).
Offers an excellent overview of European mystical activity, providing the reader with valuable context for an understanding of the rich European and English traditions of mysticism.

Webb, Diana, *Pilgrims and Pilgrimage in Medieval Europe* (London: Palgrave, 1999).
A comprehensive and accessible study of the impulse towards pilgrimage in the Middle Ages, its theories and its practices.

IV. Feminist Studies and Feminist Theory
Women in the Middle Ages

Aston, Margaret, 'Lollard Women Priests?', *Journal of Ecclesiastical History* 31, 4 (1980), pp. 441–61.
An important essay for those who are interested in the intersection between heresy and female religious activity.

Atkinson, Clarissa, *The Oldest Vocation: Christian Motherhood in the Middle Ages* (Ithaca: Cornell University Press, 1991).
A wide-ranging study of motherhood in the Middle Ages within the Christian context. Invaluable for reaching an understanding of the importance of motherhood to Margery Kempe, both as an experience and as a frame of reference throughout her life.

——, *Mystic and Pilgrim: The Book and World of Margery Kempe* (Ithaca: Cornell University Press, 1983).
An early feminist approach to the Book which provides a lively and sensitive portrayal of Margery Kempe and remains a useful place to begin when studying this text.

Baker, Derek (ed.), *Medieval Women* (Oxford: Blackwell, 1978).

Barratt, Alexandra, ' "In the Lowest Part of our Need": Julian and Medieval Gynecological Writing', in Sandra McEntire (ed.), *Julian of Norwich: A Book of Essays* (New York & London: Garland, 1998), pp. 240–56.
An important essay for contextualising the discourses of suffering as used by medieval women in their writing as a means towards empowerment.

Bynum, Caroline Walker, *Holy Feast and Holy Fast* (Berkeley: University of California Press, 1982).
A ground-breaking and seminal work to which most scholars working on medieval women are indebted, either directly or indirectly. Invaluable for its extensive overview of the complex and problematic relationship between women, suffering and food in the Middle Ages. Essential reading.

Dillon, Janet, 'Holy Women and their Confessors or Confessors and their Holy Women?' in Rosalynn Voaden (ed.), *Prophets Abroad: The Reception of Continental Holy Women in Late Medieval England* (Cambridge: D. S. Brewer, 1996), pp. 115–40.
An essay which addresses issues of power imbalances within the relationship between male ecclesiastics and their female penitents. Important for assessing Margery Kempe's often problematic relationship with the priesthood.

Finnegan, M. J., *The Women of Helfta: Scholars and Mystics* (Athens, GA & London: University of Georgia Press, 1991).
One of the few full-length examinations of the extraordinary mystical activities of the nuns at Helfta during the thirteenth century.

Gibson, Gail McMurray, *The Theatre of Devotion: East Anglian Drama and Society in the Late Middle Ages* (Chicago & London: University of Chicago Press, 1989).
An ambitious examination of drama and the visual arts alongside lay and monastic spirituality in late medieval East Anglia. Provides invaluable background material and Gibson's chapter on Margery Kempe is particularly helpful for contextualising her dramatic expressions of piety.

Green, Monica H., 'Obstetrical and Gynecological Texts in Middle English', in *Women's Healthcare in the Medieval West: Texts and Contexts* (Aldershot, Burlington, Singapore, Sydney: Ashgate, 2000), pp. 53–88.
A comprehensive and invaluable resource for those interested in female medical texts. This volume brings together many of Green's most important essays on the subject to date.

Hamington, Maurice, *Hail Mary? The Struggle for Ultimate Womanhood in Catholicism* (London: Mcrimmon Publishing, 1995).
A useful source of information which traces socio-religious attitudes towards the Virgin within Catholicism. Especially useful if read alongside Warner, Alone of All her Sex (see below).

Howell, Martha C., *Woman, Production and Patriarchy in Late Medieval Cities* (Chicago: University of Chicago Press, 1986).

Provides a bold historical reinterpretation of the contribution made by women to production in late medieval European cities.

Luango, Thomas, 'Catherine of Siena: Rewriting Female Holy Authority', in Lesley Smith and Jane Taylor (eds.), *Women, the Book, and the Godly* (Cambridge: D. S. Brewer, 1995), pp. 89–111.
Provides an excellent context for the assessment of the extent of female agency in the Middle Ages.

Morris, Bridget, *St Birgitta of Sweden* (Cambridge: D. S. Brewer, 1999).
The most recent and authoritative study of Saint Bridget. Very accessible, thorough and good for contextualising Margery Kempe's identification with the saint.

Newman, Barbara, *From Virile Woman to WomanChrist: Studies on Medieval Religion and Literature* (Philadelphia: University of Pennsylvania Press, 1995).
Ground-breaking and fascinating (if now a little dated) study of interactions of gender and religion in the context of female piety during the Middle Ages.

———, *Sister of Wisdom: Hildegarde's Theology of the Feminine* (Berkeley & Los Angeles: University of California Press, 1987).
Fruitful analysis of feminist issues pertaining to female mysticism and that of Hildegarde of Bingen in particular. Very helpful for assessing the impact and direction of Margery Kempe's own invocation of the feminine in her writing.

Power, Eileen, *Medieval Women* (Cambridge: Cambridge University Press, 1985).
A work by one of the earliest scholars to address the phalanx of 'silent' women. Fully accessible and ground-breaking, this book is one to which modern feminist historians working on women's history continue to be indebted.

Rose, Mary Beth (ed.), *Women in the Middle Ages and the Renaissance: Literary Perspectives* (Syracuse: Syracuse University Press, 1986).

Sahlin, Claire L., 'Gender and Prophetic Authority in Birgitta of Sweden's *Revelations*', in Jane Chance (ed.), *Gender and Text in the Later Middle Ages* (Gainesville: University of Florida Press, 1996), pp. 69–95.
Another good essay on the extent of agency achieved by holy women during the later Middle Ages.

Salih, Sarah, *Versions of Virginity in Late Medieval England* (Cambridge: D. S. Brewer, 2001).
A piece of excellent recent scholarship which focuses on the importance of virginity and its discourses during the time in which Margery Kempe was operating. Examines in some depth the importance of

virginity to Margery Kempe in particular and her aspirations to recapture it.

Shahar, Shulamith, *The Fourth Estate: A History of Women in the Middle Ages* (London & New York: Methuen, 1983).

Sheingorn, Pamela (ed.), *Interpreting Cultural Symbols: Saint Anne in Late Medieval Society* (Athens, GA: University of Georgia Press, 1990).

Stuard, Susan Mosher, *Women in Medieval History and Historiography* (Philadelphia: University of Pennsylvania Press, 1987).

Voaden, Rosalynn, *God's Words, Women's Voices: The Discernment of Spirits in the Writing of Late-Medieval Women Visionaries* (York: York Medieval Press, 1999).
A very important contribution to the debate on the agency of holy women in the Middle Ages. A chapter on Margery Kempe takes up a persuasive counter-argument to received opinion amongst a proportion of feminist critics.

Warner, Marina, *Alone of All her Sex: The Myth and Cult of the Virgin Mary* (London: Picador, 1990).
Provides an informative overview of the development of the Cult of the Virgin and its influence upon medieval piety.

Watt, Diane, *Secretaries of God: Women Prophets in Late Medieval and Early Modern England* (Cambridge: D. S. Brewer, 1997).
Read alongside other visionaries from the early-modern period, Watt's chapter on Margery Kempe provides an important contribution to Margery studies, adding considerably to the debate about holy women's agency and empowerment in the Middle Ages. Particularly valuable to the scholar interested in female religiosity and issues of authority generally.

———, *Medieval Women in their Communities* (Cardiff: University of Wales Press, 1997).
A series of highly accessible and thought provoking essays on how medieval women related to their communities and the effects that community had upon their lives and writing. Includes an essay on Margery Kempe by Janet Wilson (see below) which builds upon Lynn Staley's important work on Margery Kempe's subtle critique of attitudes within her own community.

Feminist Theory

Butler, Judith, *Gender Trouble: Feminism and the Subversion of Identity* (New York & London: Routledge, 1990).
A fundamental text for any student concerned with issues of gender.

Irigaray, Luce, *Spéculum of the Other Woman*, trans. Gillian C. Gill (Ithaca: Cornell University Press, 1985).

———, 'Women-Mothers, the Silent Substratum of the Social Order', in Margaret Whitford (ed.), *The Irigaray Reader* (Oxford: Blackwell, 1991), pp. 46–52.

Kristeva, Julia, '*Stabat Mater*', in Toril Moi (ed.), *The Kristeva Reader* (New York: Columbia University Press, 1986), pp. 160–86.
This essay gives an excellent insight into Margery Kempe's ambivalence towards motherhood and her deployment of its discourses as a means of gaining authority. Also helpful in its theorizing of the influence of the cult of the Virgin within the Catholic Church.

Marks, Elaine, and Isabelle de Courtivron (eds), *New French Feminisms* (New York, London, Toronto, Sydney, Tokyo: University of Massachusetts Press, 1981).

Moi, Toril, *Sexual/Textual Politics* (London & New York: Methuen, 1985).
Provides an accessible and succinct overview of the works of leading twentieth-century feminist theorists.

V. The Life and Work of Margery Kempe

Ashley, Kathleen, 'Historicizing Margery: *The Book of Margery Kempe* as Social Text', *Journal of Medieval and Early Modern Studies* 28 (1998), pp. 371–88.
Recommended reading for the placing of Margery Kempe in her historical and social context.

Beckwith, Sarah, 'A Very Material Mysticism: The Medieval Mysticism of Margery Kempe', in David Aers (ed.), *Medieval Literature: Criticism, Ideology, and History* (Brighton: Harvester Press, 1986), pp. 34–57.

———, 'Problems of Authority in Later Medieval English Mysticism: Language, Agency, and Authority in *The Book of Margery Kempe*', *Exemplaria* 4 (1992), pp. 171–200.
Both of these essays by Beckwith constitute very important contributions to Margery Kempe studies, the second forming a central contribution to the debate surrounding Margery Kempe's agency.

Craymer, Suzanne, 'Margery Kempe's Imitation of Mary Magdalene and the Digby Plays', *Mystics Quarterly*, 19 (1993), pp. 173–81.
One of a handful of essays which concentrate directly on Margery Kempe's imitatio and the only one to concentrate specifically on the links between her identification with Mary Magdalene and her performativity.

Delany, Sheila, 'Sexual Economics, Chaucer's Wife of Bath and *The Book of Margery Kempe*', in Ruth Evans and Lesley Johnson (eds), *Feminist Readings in Middle English Literature* (London: Routledge, 1994), pp. 72–87.

An astute and revealing examination of Margery Kempe who is placed alongside Chaucer's fictional Wife of Bath in this study of the possibilities open to women in the context of life within a newly commercialized society.

Dickman, S., 'Margery Kempe and the Continental Tradition of the Pious Woman', in Marion Glasscoe (ed.), *The Medieval Mystical Tradition: Papers Read at Dartington Hall, July, 1984*, Exeter Symposium III (Cambridge: D. S. Brewer, 1984), pp. 150–68.

An important contribution to insight into Margery Kempe as part of a wider European tradition of female piety and mystical practices.

Fanous, Samuel, 'Measuring the Pilgrim's Progress: Internal Emphases in *The Book of Margery Kempe*', in Denis Renevey and Christiania Whitehead (eds), *Writing Medieval Women: Female Spiritual and Textual Practices in Late Medieval England* (Cardiff: University of Wales Press, 2000), pp. 157–76.

A recent essay which is one of the few to date to address the problematics of the Book's *apparently haphazard structure. It provides a useful contribution to the debate surrounding the scribal input and ultimately argues for scribal and authorial unity.*

Farley, Mary Hardman, '"Her Own Creatur": Religion, Feminist Criticism, and the Functional Eccentricity of Margery Kempe', *Exemplaria* 11, 1 (1999), pp. 1–21.

An essay which is useful in parts but tends to place a somewhat anachronistic emphasis on Margery Kempe's behaviour as being symptomatic of a pathology.

Fienberg Nona, 'Thematics of Value in the Book of Margery Kempe', *Modern Philology* 87, 2 (1989), pp. 132–41.

A useful essay, particularly if read in conjunction with Delany (see above).

Harding, Wendy, 'Body into Text: *The Book of Margery Kempe*', in Linda Lomperis and Sarah Stanbury (eds), *Feminist Approaches to the Body in Medieval Literature* (Philadelphia: University of Pennsylvania Press, 1993), pp. 168–87.

One of a handful of critics who has recognised the importance of the female body – and the maternal body in particular – as primary discourse in Margery Kempe's Book.

Hirsch, David, *The Revelations of Margery Kempe*, Medieval and Renaissance Authors 10 (Leiden, New York, Kobenhaven, Koln: E. J. Brill, 1988).

Hirsch, John C., 'Author and Scribe in *The Book of Margery Kempe*,' *Medium Aevum* 44 (1975), pp. 145–50.

Hirsch's work provides a somewhat traditionalist view of Margery Kempe and her text, arguing for the primacy of scribal input and shaping of the Book.

Holbrook, Sue Ellen, 'Margery Kempe and Wynkyn de Worde', in Marion Glasscoe (ed.), *The Medieval Mystical Tradition in England: Papers Read at Dartington Hall, July 1987*, Exeter Symposium IV (Cambridge: D. S. Brewer, 1987), pp. 27–46.

One of the very few commentators to address the redacted text and its implications. This essay is essential for any reader interested in the impulse behind the redacted version of the text and its likely provenance.

Lavezzo, Kathy, 'Sobs and Sighs between Women: The Homoerotics of Compassion', in Louise Fradenburg and Carla Freccero (eds), *Premodern Sexualities* (New York & London: Routledge, 1996), pp. 175–98.

Offers an important and innovative 'queer reading' of the Book, *opening up several interpretive possibilities hitherto overlooked.*

Lawes, Richard, 'The Madness of Margery Kempe', in Marion Glasscoe (ed.), *The Medieval Mystical Tradition: Exeter Symposium VI*, Papers read at Charney Manor, July 1999 (Cambridge: D. S. Brewer, 1999), pp. 147–67.

A meticulously researched and presented appraisal of Margery Kempe's physchological make-up which offers a modern diagnosis of her 'condition' as a pathology – to varying levels of success.

Lochrie, Karma, *Margery Kempe and Translations of the Flesh* (Philadelphia: University of Pennsylvania Press, 1991).

A highly influential feminist reading of the Book *which constitutes essential reading for any student wishing to proceed further with this text. Lochrie's reading is probably one of the most innovative in recent years and her scholarship is now firmly established as highly influential within Margery Kempe studies.*

McAvoy, Liz Herbert, 'The Sexual Spirituality of Margery Kempe', in Susannah Chewning (ed.), *Intersections of Religion and Sexuality: The Word Made Flesh*, (Ashgate, forthcoming, 2003).

———, 'Spritual Virgin to Virgin Mother: The Confessions of Margery Kempe', *Parergon* n.s. 17, 1 (July 1999), pp. 9–44.

Two essays which examine Margery Kempe's performances of gender and sexuality as a means towards gaining authority as holy woman.

McAvoy, Liz Herbert, 'Margery's Last Child: A Refutation', *Notes and Queries* n.s. 46, 2 (June 1999), pp. 181–3.

McEntire, Sandra J. (ed.), *Margery Kempe: A Book of Essays* (New York & London: Garland, 1992).
Essential and invaluable collection of essays which examine the Book from a number of useful and illuminating theoretical perspectives. An excellent starting-point for the reader new to this text.

McSheffery, Shannon, *Gender and Heresy: Women and Men in Lollard Communities, 1420–1530* (Philadelphia: University of Pennsylvania Press, 1995).
A comprehensive assessment of the role played by gender in Lollard behavioural and doctrinal practices.

Mueller, Janel M., 'Autobiography of a New "Creatur": Female Spirituality, Selfhood, and Authorship in *The Book of Margery Kempe*', in *Women in the Middle Ages and the Renaissance*, ed. Mary Beth Rose (Syracuse: Syracuse University Press, 1986), pp. 155–82.
Provides another valuable contribution to the debate over Margery Kempe's agency and autonomy.

Partner, Nancy F., 'Reading the Book of Margery Kempe', *Exemplaria* 3 (1991), pp. 29–66.

Petroff, E. A., 'Male Confessors and Female Penitents: Possibilities for Dialogue', in *Body and Soul: Essays on Medieval Women and Mysticism* (Oxford: Oxford University Press, 1994), pp. 139–60.
This essay, appearing as it does in a volume which provides a good overview of the tradition in which Margery Kempe was attempting to operate, serves well to illuminate the nuances and possibilities for validation contained within Margery Kempe's own relationship with her various confessors.

Rees-Jones, Sarah, ' "A peler of Holy Cherch": Margery Kempe and the Bishops', in Jocelyn Wogan-Browne (ed.), *Medieval Women: Texts and Contexts in Late Medieval Britain* (Turnhout: Brepols, 2000), pp. 377–91.
An essay which takes up a stance against Margery Kempe's agency and refutes the notion of primary authorship.

Renevey, Denis, 'Margery's Performing Body: The Translation of Late Medieval Discursive Religious Practices', in Denis Renevey and Christiania Whitehead (eds), *Writing Religious Women: Female Spiritual and Textual Practices in Late Medieval England* (Cardiff: University of Wales Press, 2000), pp. 197–216.
An essay which examines the Book in the context of the primary social and historical contingencies which helped to shape medieval religious culture – and the culture of mysticism in particular. Impor-

tant for those interested in the links between Margery Kempe's piety and the anchoritic life.

Staley, Lynn, *Margery Kempe's Dissenting Fictions* (Pennsylvania: University of Pennsylvania Press, 1984).

Probably the most controversial and singular reading of the Book *to date but essential reading for the serious scholar intent on addressing the issue of authorship and authority.*

Stargardt, Ute, 'The Beguines of Belgium, the Dominican Nuns of Germany, and Margery Kempe', in J. Heffernan (ed.), *The Popular Literature of Medieval England* (Knoxville: University of Tennessee Press, 1985), pp. 277–313.

Uhlman, Diane, 'The comfort of Voice, the Solace of Script: Orality and Literacy in *The Book of Margery Kempe*', *Studies in Philology*, 91 (1994), pp. 50–69.

Addresses the problems raised by the intervention of the scribe in Margery Kempe's writing and offers a useful appraisal of the extent to which this text can be considered to be a reflection of Margery's orality.

Weissman, Hope Phyllis, 'Margery Kempe in Jerusalem: *Hysterica Compassio* in the Late Middle Ages', in Mary Carruthers and Elizabeth Kirk (eds), *Acts of Interpretation: The Text in its Contexts 700–1600* (Oklahoma: Pilgrim Books, 1982), pp. 201–17.

An important essay which places Margery's eccentric behaviour within the context of accepted practices within medieval piety and focuses – albeit briefly – upon some of the motherhood issues dealt with in more detail by the editor of this current volume.

Wilson, Janet, 'Communities of Dissent: The Secular and Ecclesiastical Communities of Margery Kempe's *Book*', in Diane Watt (ed.), *Medieval Women in their Communities* (Cardiff: Cardiff University Press, 1997), pp. 155–85).

An essay of considerable interest which examines the Book *in terms of its marginal status alongside the marginality of its author. Wilson also places it in the wider context of the diversity of East Anglian piety.*

Index

Meech, Sandford Brown
The Book of Margery Kempe (ed.,
with Allen) 1 n. 3, 5 n. 12, 6 n.
14, 11 n. 23, 12 n. 25, 13 n. 29,
22 n. 41, 79 n. 2, 94 n. 22
Methley, Richard 6
Meun, Jean de
The Romance of the Rose (with
Guillaume de Lorris) 1
mimesis, Margery's use of
attitudes to female sexuality 107–8,
118–22
attitudes to motherhood 107–8,
112–18
Moi, Toril 108 n. 7, 109 n. 11, 114
Mondeville, Henri de 123
Morris, Bridget 24 n. 45
motherhood
contemporary attitudes to 108–9
Margery's mimetic adherence to
107–8, 112–18
discourses of 25–6
the birth of Margery's first child
31–3
the conception of Margery's last
child 33–5
the conversion of Margery's son
49–51
curing the woman with
post-partum sickness 52–3
the devotional doll 41–4
imitatio Maria at Jerusalem
35–41
vision of the Nativity 44–6
vision of the Passion 46–8
Mount Calvary 36 n. 8, 37, 38, 39, 40,
115, 120, 121, 123
Mount Grace, priory of 5–6
Mount of Olives 47
Mount Zion 40
Mueller, Janel M. 13 n. 27
music, heavenly 54, 72
Myrour to Lewde Men and Wymmen, A
(anon.) 19–20
mystical ecstasy 15, 54, 121
mysticism, female *see* female
mysticism, continental tradition of

Nativity, Margery's vision of 44–6
Nelson, Venetia 20 n. 37

Newman, Barbara 2 n. 5, 14 n. 31, 23
44
Noffke, Suzanne 106 n. 4
Norton, John 6
Norwich, Margery's visits to 3, 22–3,
91–4, 123
see also Julian of Norwich

Ohler, Norbert 19 n. 35
Oldcastle, John 16, 86 n. 10, 88
ontology 113
oral authority, Margery's search for
91–4
orgasm, female 121

Palm Sunday 48
Passion of Our Lord 36–41, 44, 46–8,
68, 71, 86, 96, 120–21, 129, 130,
131
Paul, Saint 1, 2, 34, 69, 83, 93, 108,
110, 117
penance, bodily 31, 55–6, 59–60, 73–4,
127
Pentney Abbey 78
Pepwell, Henry 6, 7, 127 n. 2, 128 n. 5,
131 n. 9
Petroff, E.A. 109 n. 12
phallic model 122 n. 35
pilgrimages
Margery's 18–19, 20–21
see also Beverley, Margery's
trial at; Jerusalem, Margery's
pilgrimage to; Leicester,
Margery's trial at; Prussia;
Rome, Margery's visit to; Spain,
Margery's pilgrimage to; York,
Margery's trial at
religious controversy surrounding
19–21
Plato
Timaeus 124
plenary indulgence 40, 41 n. 12,
130–31
Porete, Marguerite 6 n. 13, 26
post-partum sickness
curing the woman with 52–3
Margery's, following birth of first
child 3, 5, 31–3, 109–12
Potter, R. 3 n. 9
Power, Eileen 112 n. 16

Already published titles in this series

Christine de Pizan's Letter of Othea to Hector, *Jane Chance*, 1990

The Writings of Margaret of Oingt, Medieval Prioress and Mystic, *Renate Blumenfeld-Kosinski*, 1990

Saint Bride and her Book: Birgitta of Sweden's Revelations, *Julia Bolton Holloway*, 1992

The Memoirs of Helene Kottanner (1439–1440), *Maya Bijvoet Williamson*, 1998

The Writings of Teresa de Cartagena, *Dayle Seidenspinner-Núñez*, 1998

Julian of Norwich: *Revelations of Divine Love* and *The Motherhood of God*: an excerpt, *Frances Beer*, 1998

Hrotsvit of Gandersheim: A Florilegium of her Works, *Katharina M. Wilson*, 1998

Hildegard of Bingen: On Natural Philosophy and Medicine: Selections from *Cause et Cure, Margret Berger*, 1999

Women Saints' Lives in Old English Prose, *Leslie A. Donovan*, 1999

Angela of Foligno's Memorial, *Cristina Mazzoni*, 2000

The Letters of the Rožmberk Sisters, *John M. Klassen*, 2001

The Life of Saint Douceline, a Beguine of Provence, *Kathleen Garay and Madeleine Jeay*, 2001

Agnes Blannbekin, Viennese Beguine: Life and Revelations, *Ulrike Wiethaus*, 2002

Women of the *Gilte Legende*: A Selection of Middle English Saints Lives, *Larissa Tracy*

Mechthild of Magdeburg: Selections from *The Flowing Light of the Godhead*, *Elizabeth A. Andersen*